Landscape Archaeology
and GIS

Landscape Archaeology
and GIS

Henry Chapman

TEMPUS

For Sam

First published 2006

Tempus Publishing Limited
The Mill, Brimscombe Port,
Stroud, Gloucestershire, GL5 2QG
www.tempus-publishing.com

British Library Cataloguing in Publication Data.
A catalogue record for this book is available from the British Library.

ISBN 0 7524 3603 1

Typesetting and origination by Tempus Publishing Limited
Printed in Great Britain

Contents

Foreword

Henry has been our main surveyor on *Time Team* since 2001 over the last 80 programmes and he and his GPS pole have become familiar items to those of us regulars on the programme. With his sophisticated surveying kit, Henry enables us to fix the positions of trenches, finds and structures and to lay out the areas for geophysical and topographical survey.

I occasionally take time to ask Henry how many satellites there are overhead and how the survey work is going, but it all seems rather miraculous to me that military satellites can be used for archaeological surveying – real 'swords into ploughshares' stuff. But of course this is only the beginning of a long process. Once the data are gathered there is all the manipulation on computer to produce useful information for us. Much of this these days is related to GIS – Geographical Information Systems. Older readers will remember how maps used to be drawn with drawing boards, plastic film and tracing paper, and rows of clogged up pens. Now this work is done on computers using GIS and a great deal of additional information can be delivered as a result.

This book is about much more than what modern gismos can do to help in archaeological survey work. Henry looks at what landscape archaeology is – I feel close to this as, with Trevor Rowley, I invented the term back in 1974 – and how the study of the landscape can be enhanced with GIS. This discussion is wide and many related aspects of landscape archaeology are examined.

This book will provide the best one-stop resource for current practice in GIS for archaeology for some time to come.

I am sure, for *Time Team* fans and others wishing to learn more about practical archaeological methods, this book will enhance knowledge of GPS, GIS and landscape archaeology practice, and I recommend it enthusiastically.

Professor Mick Aston

Acknowledgements

This book is the result of a decade of research and consultancy work on a wide range of archaeological landscapes throughout the UK and abroad. During this time I have been fortunate to work with a vast range of individuals without whom this book would not have been possible. The majority of the examples outlined have resulted from projects generously funded by English Heritage, *Time Team* and English Nature during my employment at the Universities of Hull and Birmingham. Discussions with Professor Mick Aston and Guy de la Bédoyère provided the impetus for this book and thanks are due to Tim Taylor (Series Producer) and Philip Clarke (Executive Producer) of *Time Team* for involving me in the programme and for their continued support over the past six years, providing me with the opportunity to work on a wide variety of sites and with a broad range of individuals. I am also indebted to ESRI, Trimble and the Ordnance Survey who have been extremely supportive over the years.

I am particularly grateful for the support from and discussion with a number of past and present colleagues and other individuals including Stewart Ainsworth (English Heritage), Raysan Al-Kubaisi (*Time Team*), Ruth Atkinson (Humber Archaeology Partnership), Dr Tim Bellerby (University of Hull), Dr Nòra Bermingham, Dr James Brasington (University of Cambridge), Dr Jane Bunting (University of Hull), Ian Carstairs (Carstairs Countryside Trust), Keith Challis (University of Birmingham), Dr James Cheetham (Wessex Archaeology), Dr Mark Dinnin, Dr Steve Ellis (University of Hull), Neil Emmanuel (*Time Team*), Helen Fenwick (University of Hull), Dr Graham Ferrier (University of Hull), William Fletcher (Suffolk County Council), Dr Benjamin Gearey (University of Birmingham), Dr Chris Gaffney (GSB Prospection), Professor Vince Gaffney (University of Birmingham), John Gater (GSB Prospection), Dr Mark Gillings (University of Leicester), Keith Hofgartner (Trimble), Dr Helen Keeley (English Heritage), Tim Kohler (English Nature), Roy Laming (ESRI UK), Dr Malcolm Lillie (University of Hull), Dr Marcos Llobera (University of Washington), Dr

Gary Lock (University of Oxford), Dick Middleton (University of Hull), Keith Miller (English Heritage), Dr Heike Neumann, Ian Panter (English Heritage), Dr Julian Richards (University of York), Dinah Saich (South Yorkshire Archaeology Service), Gavin Thomas (RSPB), Professor Robert Van de Noort (University of Exeter), Dr Nicki Whitehouse (Queen's University Belfast) and Steve Wilkes (University of Birmingham). I have also benefited from working with numerous other individuals from a range of institutions and field units across the country.

Additional material for illustrations was supplied by GSB Prospection and *Time Team* (figures *10*, *17* and *27*). The aerial photograph presented in figure *8* was taken by Neil Mitchell (APS UK). Colour plate *2* was provided by Keith Challis and figures *12* and *16* were provided by Emma Wood. *Colour plate 25* and the texture for *colour plate 24* were generated by Raysan Al-Kubaisi.

1

Landscape archaeology and GIS

INTRODUCTION

There can be no question that Geographical Information System technology (also known as Geographical Information Science or GIS) has already made a tremendous impact on archaeology and that this impact continues to increase. Its use has both influenced, and been influenced by, all areas of archaeological research and practice. GIS is commonly used within data repositories internationally, at both the regional and national levels, since they provide a spatial component to the more traditional database structures. It is also common within archaeological research, both as a data management tool and as a methodology in its own right. Clearly, GIS is important to archaeological research but to what extent does it remain a basis for holding and sorting the information gleaned from field archaeology, and to what extent does it provide a new archaeological method in itself?

This book addresses these questions in relation to landscape archaeology. It considers the ways in which the exciting 'toolbox' offered by GIS technology can be used to provide new ways of addressing the questions of landscape archaeology, testing old hypotheses and generating new ones. It is focused towards a general archaeological audience. This audience includes those who already use GIS, but wish to expand their landscape archaeology functionality, and those landscape archaeologists who require a tool to assist in some of the difficulties encountered, such as the visibility of archaeological remains on the ground due to later activity.

This book differs from many on the subject in that it is structured around the particular needs of landscape archaeology, rather than around the tools provided by GIS. These needs include elements of cartography and map analyses (including the pitfalls encountered when working with spatial data), in addition

1 Some of the sites mentioned in the text. 1) Giant's Grave, Feltar, Shetland, 2) Loch Migdale, Sutherland, Highlands, 3) Applecross, Wester Ross, 4) Drumlanrig, Dumfries and Galloway, 5) Rudston, East Yorkshire, 6) Holderness, East Yorkshire, 7) North Ferriby, East Yorkshire, 8) Thorne Moors, South Yorkshire, 9) Sutton Common, South Yorkshire, 10) Hatfield Moors, South Yorkshire, 11) Carsington Pasture, Derbyshire, 12) Confluence of the rivers Trent and Soar, Nottinghamshire, 13) Glendon Hall, Northamptonshire, 14) Beaudesert Castle, Henley in Arden, Warwickshire, 15) Conderton Camp, Gloucestershire, 16) Chesham Bois, Hertfordshire, 17) Bath, 18) Esher, Surrey, 19) Meare, Somerset, 20) Dinnington, Somerset, 21) Breamore, Hampshire, 22), Cock Hill, Blackpatch, West Sussex, 23) Shorncliffe Redoubt, Folkestone, Kent, 24) Green Island, Poole Harbour, Dorset, 25) Merrivale, Dartmoor, Devon, 26) Gear Farm, Cornwall

to remotely-sensed data (particularly aerial photography) and features on the ground such as earthworks. It draws on varied examples (*1*) to provide practical solutions for obtaining relevant data efficiently, and for processing this data whilst avoiding some of the potential errors that may be encountered.

Effectively then, this is a handbook for the use of GIS within landscape archaeology, providing best practice information, case studies and ideas for developing new methods.

WHAT IS LANDSCAPE ARCHAEOLOGY?

The term 'landscape archaeology' means many things to many people, and consequently requires some clarification within the context of this book. According to the Collins *Dictionary of Archaeology* (Bahn 1992) landscape archaeology may be defined as:

> … an approach, especially in archaeological survey, where the unit of analysis is the artefact rather than the site … [It] recognises that many of the material consequences of human behaviour are ephemeral and will not conform to standard definitions of sites, and documents the distribution of humanly-modified materials across the landscape.

Fundamentally, landscape archaeology is a term commonly used to characterise those areas of archaeological research and interpretation that consider the landscape as opposed to the site, the interrelationship between sites, and the physical spaces separating them (*2*). In essence, information from all areas of archaeological research may be used to examine archaeological landscapes, though the methods that are most commonly used include cartographic study, documentary research, fieldwalking and survey. However, three principal, though overlapping, philosophical approaches have been applied to landscape archaeological research.

The first has mirrored landscape history, approaching the subject from the perspective of regression by the removal of later, datable layers of human activity in order to reveal earlier ones. The methods by which this has been approached include the identification of clues within the present landscape, such as idiosyncrasies of field morphology, in addition to cartographic evidence. However, other archaeological skills have served to enhance research, including earthwork survey, aerial photographic analysis and fieldwalking. The combination of methods has often supplied the key to providing a wide range of clues, identifying the complex palimpsest of past activity that characterises

2 Merrivale stone rows, Dartmoor. Landscape archaeology is about exploring sites and their landscape setting, but also the relationship between different landscape features

our landscape today (e.g. Aston 1985, Bowden 1999, Hoskins 1955, Muir 2000, Ordnance Survey 1973, Rackham 1986, Riley 1980, Stoertz 1997, Taylor 1984, Wilson 1982, Wood 1963). This approach may be termed as 'landscape analysis', based upon considerations of observable data and investigating trends within it.

A second approach has also concentrated on the physical remains of the past, but through the scientific reconstruction of the changing environment through time based on the examination of botanical remains (*3*). Much of the history of this discipline extends to the work of Harry Godwin who, based in Cambridge during the 1960s, produced some of the earliest innovative work in the reconstruction of past landscapes and environments using microfossil remains of plants, particularly of pollen (Godwin 1975). More recently a complex range of microfossils and macrofossils have been studied in order to obtain a picture of earlier landscapes, including pollen, plant macrofossils, seeds, diatoms, testate amoebae and insects. Samples for analysis may be extracted from a particular on-site deposit or as part of a sequence within the landscape. Furthermore, once dated, analysed samples can begin to give various levels of information about the local environment and the types of activities that might have been going on at different periods.

3 Collecting samples for palaeoenvironmental analyses using coring equipment

A more recent development has concentrated upon the interpretation of the qualitative aspects of archaeological landscapes. The approach has focused on elements of experience, the point of departure being that maps and plans of landscapes are an abstraction of the world and consequently cannot be relied upon alone when attempting to interpret what it is to be within a landscape. Through narrative approaches and other techniques borrowed from the social sciences, the exploration of archaeological landscapes has been enabled through the study of the interrelationship between monuments themselves, and between monuments and natural features (e.g. Bender 1993, Bradley 1993, 2000, Tilley 1994). Typically, sensual perception of landscapes has been paramount to interpretations, with plurality often being favoured.

So, landscape archaeology is a multi-faceted discipline with differing philosophies and contrasting methodologies. The various paradigms that fall under the landscape archaeology label provide various avenues to both archaeological interpretation and the management of the past landscapes. In this book, landscape archaeology is taken to include all of these themes in the broadest sense, drawing on these three principal philosophical approaches and within the various spatial resolutions at which landscape may be examined; from the extra-site locale, to the wider, multiple-site region.

WHAT IS GIS?

As mentioned previously, GIS stands for Geographical Information Systems and, more broadly, for Geographical Information Science. This is the name given to a range of software programmes featuring spatial databases. GIS is part of a wider bracket of technologies known as Spatial Information Systems, or SIS, and increasingly the boundaries between GIS and other software, such as Computer Aided Design (CAD), are becoming blurred. However, let us begin with some definitions.

> An organized collection of computer hardware, software, geographic data, and personnel designed to efficiently capture, store, update, manipulate, analyze, and display all forms of geographically referenced information.
> ESRI 1995 (glossary)

> A GIS is a sophisticated database management system designed for the acquisition, manipulation, visualisation, management and display of spatially referenced (or geographic) data.
> Aldenderfer 1996, 4

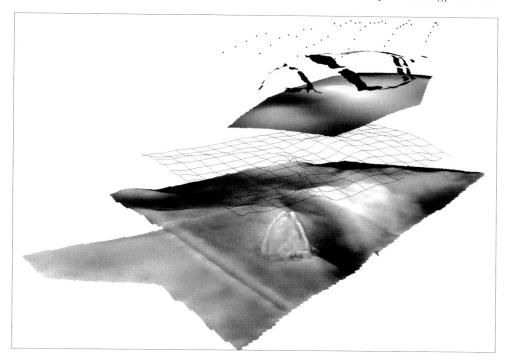

4 Layers of data within a GIS incorporating both rasters and vectors

> ... GIS is increasingly being seen as much as a place to think as a simple data management and mapping tool.
>
> Gillings and Goodrick 1996.

GIS can be interpreted in a number of different ways though, fundamentally, the name GIS describes a range of software packages displaying the common abilities to store, manage, manipulate, analyse and display spatially referenced information (*4*).

Traditionally, GIS software packages have been divided into two types on the basis of data management: vector systems and raster systems. The former stores data in relation to points (or nodes), lines (or arcs) and closed polygons. The storage of such data reflects the mathematical discipline of topology, whereby the relationship between points is important rather than their true positions. The latter considers space in terms of cells, dividing a digital surface into regular blocks that can each be given a value or attribute that describes it. For example, cells may be labelled with information attributing to colour or shade, as is often used for two-dimensional images or maps, or by numerical values, such as heights, to provide a third dimension. Within more advanced GIS packages the representation of height in addition to Cartesian data means that topographic maps may be created. The nature of data storage, however, means that the third dimension is stored as an attribute representing height, unlike the continuous scales in the other two dimensions. As a result such models are considered as 2.5 dimensional (2.5D). The value of cell-based modelling of this kind is that different types of surfaces may be generated and compared mathematically in order to create new models.

In application, the differences between raster and vector GIS are not always so clearly defined, with models typically containing data of both types. Both types of data management provide the potential for generating, manipulating and analysing digital landscape surfaces, or Digital Elevation Models (DEMs), with the main limitation being the complexity of the software itself. Further, they both have the potential for being overlain with other multiple layers of data of different types. However, raster data structures require greater computer memory, although they have the advantage of being more flexible for further analysis. It is possible to convert data between the two data types, although the potential for generating error within such procedures has been highlighted (e.g. Van der Knapp 1992).

Digital mapping was first introduced by Waldo Tobler with the 'map in map out' (MIMO) model that first applied computers to cartography (Centre for Spatial Analysis, University College London – http://www.casa.ucl.ac.uk/gistimeline). The first true GIS was created in 1962 in Canada and was called the Canadian Geographic Information System (CGIS). It was developed in response to two factors – the growth in electronic computer technology, and the increased complexities of life that needed to be considered within the framework of public and private sector decision-making. Two years later a similar system was created in the USA called MIDAS that began processing data on natural resources. At this time the focus of GIS was to manage developments and infrastructure expansion, and to aid in the planning process (Bernhardsen 1992). By the end of the 1960s the development of GIS had led to the creation of commercially based software companies, beginning with the Environmental Systems and Research Institute (ESRI), followed by others (Centre for Spatial Analysis, University College London – http://www.casa.ucl.ac.uk/gistimeline). The development of the microprocessor in 1971-2 increased the functionality of computers. A gradual replacement of manual cartographic work and the development of GIS followed this during the 1970s and 1980s (Bernhardsen 1992). In 1981 ARC/INFO was first launched by ESRI. Throughout the 1980s new products and the creation of research initiatives reflected the growth in GIS. In 1987 the publication of the 'Chorley Report' (Committee of enquiry into the handling of geographic information 1987) appears to have fostered the development of GIS within the

UK, although it never led to the establishment of a national initiative as it had done in the USA. Rather, it led to a series of regional research programmes funded by the Economic and Social Research Council (ESRC) (Centre for Spatial Analysis, University College London – http://www.casa.ucl.ac.uk/gistimeline). It was in the same year that the *International Journal of Geographical Information Systems* (Taylor and Francis) was first published.

ARCHAEOLOGY AND GIS

Harris and Lock (1990) provide a documentary of the early development of GIS within archaeology. The first use of GIS within an archaeological context was in the 1980s in North America where it was used to predict archaeological site location within a management context (Kohler and Parker 1986, *cf.* Gillings and Wise 1998). Interest in GIS and its potential within archaeology appears to have emerged in 1985 at conferences organised by the Society for American Archaeology. The first included papers relating to the analysis of intra-site distribution using GIS (presented by Gill and Howes), and the use of GIS for regional archaeological research (presented by Kvamme). The second conference saw papers on methods and principles. The following year a third conference, the *National Workshop on Microcomputers in Archaeology*, saw papers on the potential of GIS for archaeological research and data management (presented by Kvamme) and on the availability of appropriate software (one presented by Ferguson and another by Miller) (reported on in Harris and Lock 1990).

Within the UK the genesis of interest in GIS appears to have occurred at the same time as in the USA, but the uptake was faster within geographical rather than archaeological study. The initial interest in relation to archaeology was in the mid-1980s and was focused upon the computerisation of spatial data at a regional level for archiving, education and research, and to aid decision-making in the planning process (Harris 1986). By the later 1980s the potential of GIS within archaeology in the UK had been broadened to include 2.5D modelling with archaeological data draped over digital terrain models (Harris 1988). The development of GIS continued into different archaeological applications over the succeeding years (Harris and Lock 1990). More recently, such developments have merged the distinctions between Computer Aided Design (CAD) and GIS, and the wider issues of general data management, compatibility and storage (e.g. Gillings and Wise 1998) have come to the fore. The use of GIS within archaeology has become widespread at all levels and within all sub-disciplines. This has been reflected over the past few years, for example, by the growth of the GISarch e-mail discussion list (http://www.jiscmail.ac.uk/lists/gisarch.

html). It has also been reflected in an expansion of archaeological GIS into other computer disciplines (*cf.* Gillings and Goodrick 1996).

Archaeological research may be split into three main areas: methods, interpretation and management. These have been used to identify the main three themes of research into GIS within the archaeological context, even though many projects combine different aims together (e.g. Chartrand *et al.* 1993). A further theme of *spatial statistics* has also been developed that has been closely linked to management, but dominated to a greater extent by predictive modelling, particularly of site location (Harris and Lock 1995).

GIS procedure and archaeology

The first theme, relating to methods, is often referred to as GIS procedure (e.g. Savage 1990), and is primarily concerned with the accuracy of results from studies using GIS, often at an algorithmic level (e.g. Kvamme 1990). The sphere of GIS procedure is relatively indistinct in relation to archaeology, as it extends into other analyses using GIS. For example, studies examining the potential error within GIS algorithms will apply to archaeology and other disciplines, providing a wider literature base. Themes of research have included methods of raw data sampling in relation to accurate surface generation (Fletcher and Spicer 1988), processes of surface generation from various data sources and using different algorithms, and measuring accuracy (e.g. Kvamme 1990, Haigh 1993, Carrara *et al.* 1997, Gao 1997, Lopez 1997, Voigtmann *et al.* 1997), and the error within the algorithms used for further analyses and ways of approaching it (e.g. Fisher 1993, De Floriani and Magillo 1994, De Floriani *et al.* 1994, Puppo and Marzano 1997). Other work has been more ambiguous, falling within the spheres of GIS procedure and other themes such as interpretation (e.g. Wheatley and Gillings 2000). Many such papers present a new method, using an example to present the method. For example, Lake *et al.* (1998) outlined a GIS procedure that tailored the basic software in order to speed up analyses. While this may be considered to fall within the sub-heading of GIS procedure, the process was developed and presented as a way of quantifying archaeological landscape interpretation. It seems that the boundaries, particularly between procedure and the other two main spheres of GIS work outlined below, are extremely blurred.

GIS and landscape archaeology

The need to obtain meaning from data is fundamental to the study of archaeology and so a level of interpretation is always required. Approaches to understanding archaeological landscapes may be considered in relation to three main trends, loosely reflecting historical developments in theory. The first of these may be termed *normative*; essentially classifying data according to common patterns;

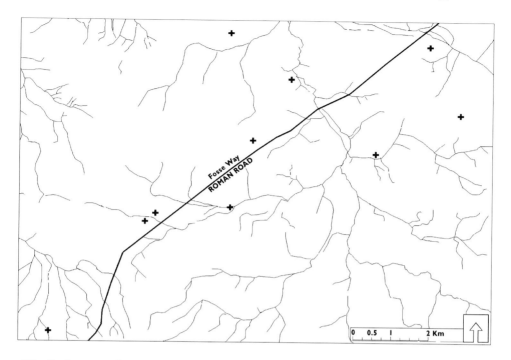

5 Distribution map of Roman-period villa sites along the Fosse Way, Somerset

creating 'cultures' that reflect 'normal' behaviour (e.g. Piggott 1968). Within landscape studies the principal traditional tool for this has been the distribution map (5), used to describe and interpret spatial patterns of similar artefacts or assemblages, and how they change through time. Interpretation from such sources is typically carried out by creating theories to explain the boundaries of these 'cultures' in order to understand changes seen in the archaeological record (e.g. Piggott 1968). This approach may be criticised for being descriptive and deterministic (e.g. Binford 1964), especially as the classification of the 'cultures' forms essentially false boundaries between them, limited to the chosen parameters and without consideration of anomalous features. The creation of false boundaries typically determines interpretations of change based upon either a migration of population or diffusion of ideas, rather than upon other theories such as evolution. Consequently, conclusions typically take the form of descriptions.

The second generalising theme in landscape interpretation relates to some of the developments of the *New Archaeology*, and is often referred to as *processual* (*cf.* Clarke 1978). Themes include the requirement to become 'scientific' in approach, to construct models to explain the archaeological record rather than to describe it, and to add other levels of data including those from anthropo-logical analogies and environmental work. Borrowing from the other social sciences, popular approaches stem from the creation and testing of theories to construct robust conclusions. Much of this work has grown from positivist reasoning – testing hypotheses to create new ones on the basis of generalisation. Within landscape archaeology, the main developments have been in relation to environmental factors and the integration of 'scientific' methods of palaeoeco-logical reconstruction such as palynology. This type of approach may be criticised for a number of reasons, primarily that the problem of inferring interpretation from archaeological data still required a jump from the results to generalisation (*cf.* Popper 1992). Similarly the parameters that could be studied were still a construct of their survival and were therefore not real. Many critics of this type of approach indicate that the systems created are deterministic, particularly environmentally, in relation to archaeological landscapes (e.g. Bradley 1984).

The third theme is commonly referred to as *theoretical*, in contrast to 'scientific'. It reflects a more humanistic view of the archaeological record. This has been applied to landscape archaeology in such a way that it has developed into a discipline in its own right (e.g. Tilley 1994). Central to this has been the presumption that landscapes are imbued with meaning (*cf.* Cosgrove 1989), and that this meaning transcends economics and filters into all activities. As such, landscapes are seen as more than merely a surface that archaeology rests upon (or within), but rather as interactive platforms for human experience. The landscape is constantly recreated through physical and metaphysical constructions that constantly alter the relationship between it and those people who engage in activities within it. The physical constructions may be measured, at least in part, through archaeological investigation, and it is on the basis of these features that meaning is sought. However, it has been argued that the same landscape can be perceived in different ways by different people or from different perspectives (Meinig 1979, Tuan 1979, Bender 1992).

Landscapes have been classified in a number of ways. Fundamental to many of these has been Tuan's (1977) distinction between place (where activity occurs) and space (the area between places where paths reside). The central themes within landscape theory are underpinned by the definition of landscape (*cf.* Olwig 1993). Tilley (1996) summarised the relationship between archaeology and landscape in four ways: (1) as '… a set of relationships between named locales' (p. 161); (2) to be '… experienced and known through the movement of the human body in space and through time' (p. 162); (3) as '… a primary medium of socialisation' (p. 162); and (4) creating 'self-identity' by controlling knowledge and thereby influencing power structures (p. 162). The key principle is that of experience, and thus studies of archaeological landscapes have been based upon attempting to replicate the experience of 'Being-in-the-world' while trying to reconstruct the dialectic of the existential 'Being' (Tilley 1994: 12). The primary method of measuring experience (if measuring is a suitable word) is through analysing visibility patterns. For example, Thomas (1993) investigated the visual impact of monuments, particularly around Avebury, suggesting themes of inclusion and exclusion (similar to Tilley's fourth point, mentioned above). Devereux (1991) analysed the spatial relationships between monuments and topography at Avebury by investigating their visual relationships. Similarly, Tilley (1994) investigated three archaeological landscapes through a narrative and photographic essay and by recording patterns of intervisibility between monuments.

Work involving the interpretation of past landscapes revolves around what may be defined as the two areas of perception and cognition (van Leusen 1999). Perception can be defined in terms of landscape awareness and includes feelings of being within the landscape. Cognition within landscape archaeology can be defined as knowledge of the landscape that influences perception (Zubrow 1994). For example, cultural or social implications of a certain place may influence its significance within a landscape and may form a completely different perception of the environment; the imbuing of meaning upon landscape and extracting meaning from it.

GIS provides a forum that enables multiple disciplinary studies and can therefore assist in interpretation (e.g. Potts *et al.* 1996). The potential for reconstructing past landscapes within a digital framework allows for the possibility of stripping back the temporal layers to provide a basis for quantifiable analysis. However, the specific application of GIS to landscape archaeology lacks the historical development of the archaeological discipline, being a relatively new technique; 'in GIS the concept of theory is less mature' (Zubrow 1990a: 69). Perhaps as a consequence of this the divisions between approaches are less pronounced and studies tend to span two or more of the paradigms described above. Interpretation within GIS may, however, be divided in terms of levels of sophistication.

The least sophisticated interpretative models act in a similar way to the distribution plots seen within work characterised as normative archaeology. However, the advantage of GIS is its capability to display multiple layers of data together such that correlation with other forms of data is often used as a tool for understanding (e.g. Middleton and Winstanley 1993, Van de Noort and Ellis 1995, 1997, 1998, 1999, 2000). More sophisticated models use algorithms to provide information about the topographic surface, thereby allowing the GIS to generate data rather than merely to correlate external datasets. For example, distance to resources may be calculated in order to understand relationships between different data sources (e.g. van Leusen 1993), or sites may be examined in relation

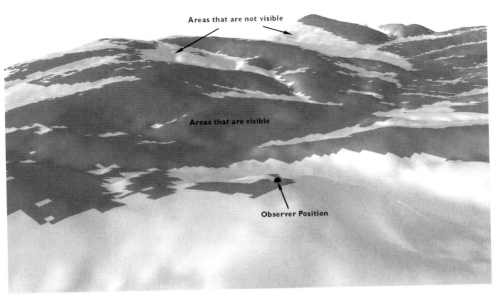

6 Viewshed functions calculate which cells within a DEM can be seen from a given location or locations. Here, the visible areas are shown in a darker grey

to elements such as aspect or slope angle. Such analyses are often descriptive rather than directly interpretative, forming a common basis for locational predictive modelling (mentioned above), but also acting as a foundation for other methods of interpretation.

More sophisticated approaches tend to be based around two main elements: visual analysis and cost-surface analysis. The most common approach is through the creation of viewsheds (*6*), and the analysis of what is visible from a given position in much the same way as is done by Tilley (1994) and others on the ground (e.g. Exon *et al.* 2001).

Part of the reason for this is the potential for GIS to quantify visibility (*cf.* Wheatley 1995, Lock and Harris 1996, Fisher *et al.* 1997, Lake *et al.* 1998, van Leusen 1999, see chapter 5). Some approaches combine the viewsheds from several positions in order to analyse distributions of monuments. For example, Lock and Harris (1996) argued that Neolithic long barrows in the Danebury area represented highly visible territorial markers because their calculated viewsheds did not overlap. Cumulative viewshed analysis has grown as a sub-context of visual analysis and this was characterised by Wheatley (1995). This is a technique that combines the viewsheds from several monuments, investigating recurrence of visible areas in order to assess visual qualities of monuments from a statistical perspective. This type of approach has been expanded to assess the validity of empirical interpretations by the introduction of random points from which to generate viewsheds (Fisher *et al.* 1997). In this way interpretations based on monument positions (chosen *places*) may be compared to those from other areas (random *space*). This approach was extended by Lake *et al.* (1998) who achieved such an analysis by 'tailoring' a GIS software package to enable automated analyses. This process allowed for the comparative quantitative investigation of viewsheds from a large sample of cells within the model, in order to assess whether an archaeological site might have been located due to its significantly higher visibility.

A second approach towards providing insight into the interpretation of past landscape from a cognitive perspective is the creation and analysis of 'cost-surfaces' (Wheatley 1993, Stead 1995, Gaffney *et al.* 1996, Maschner 1996, van Leusen 1999, Bell and Lock 2000, De Silva and Pizziolo 2001). This technique is based upon the possibility of measuring the effort it takes to cross an area of the DEM. For example, an area of flat land would be easier to cross than a steep area. A cost-surface generates different values for each of the cells making up the surface based on whichever parameters are chosen; though commonly slope is a significant factor. A cost-surface can then be used to find the path between two points on the surface that encounters the least effort. Such approaches have been used to investigate how past landscapes may have been perceived (e.g. Wheatley 1993, Stead 1995), and to define and explain routes, such as the Ridgeway extending across the southern chalklands of England (Bell and Lock 2000).

A combination of both visual and cost-surface analyses has been used on a number of occasions to provide a broader basis for interpretation (e.g. Gaffney *et al.* 1996, Lock and Harris 1996, Chapman 2003). Each of these methods outlined here in relation to the themes of GIS and landscape interpretation is expanded upon in chapters 5 and 6.

A disadvantage of past and current approaches to interpretative landscape archaeology is that there is a general desire to produce testable models and theories (e.g. Zubrow 1990b, Lake *et al.* 1998). Although repeatable and testable experiments are useful in terms of positivist theory (e.g. Bell 1994), the fundamental reasoning of post-processual interpretation lies beyond the need for them, with criticisms levelled towards such processes. For example, past populations could not analyse a landscape to find the most suitable position in terms of visibility and so there may have been better, unknown sites. Further, such theories exclude the influence of cultural factors that may equally determine the positioning of a site. GIS has also been criticised for its abstract nature, in terms of being environmentally deterministic (*cf.* Gaffney and van Leusen 1995). It works by assessing measurable aspects such as slope, aspect and distance, and so it may be argued that this capability will determine interpretative processes.

However, as Llobera (1996) noted, such a criticism may lie in the semantic confusion of the words 'environmental' and 'deterministic', and may therefore be over-simplifying the role of the user. Rather, Llobera argued that GIS should be seen as a heuristic tool for exploring the possibilities of social theory, with the abstract social theories 'translated' into GIS approaches. This conforms to trends within non-archaeological GIS approaches elsewhere that aim for increased conceptual sophistication by adding a social perspective to models, including the subjectivity of the observer (Couclelis 1999).

GIS and Cultural Resource Management (CRM)

CRM is also referred to as archaeological resource management (van Leusen 1995) and is commonly associated with site location modelling (Savage 1990). CRM covers the majority of professional applications of GIS and is often publicly funded. The many processes and activities encountered within this broad title may be categorised into three main themes: recording, protection and management.

Recording archaeological resources encompasses both the classification of sites and landscapes and their archiving. In relation to GIS, this theme includes aspects of database design, creation and management (e.g. Stine and Lanter 1990), site categorisation and the digital archive (Williams *et al*. 1990, *cf*. Gillings and Wise 1998). Such work is typically focused on the values and caveats of using GIS as a data curation, management and display tool (e.g. Guillot and Leroy 1995). Trends within this area of CRM highlight the various ways of approaching these three themes, but acknowledge the common value of GIS for the management of large quantities of data.

The second area of CRM, which may be termed 'protection', is a broader concept encompassing mitigation strategies for threatened archaeology such as preservation by record, preservation *in situ*, and rescue excavation, and is governed largely by documents such as PPG16 (Department of the Environment 1990). This aspect of CRM involves the decision-making processes by which a threatened site is managed. GIS studies addressing this aspect of CRM often involve more complex modelling techniques, typically exploiting their ability to model possible outcomes, such as site distributions, in one area based upon trends identified from empirical observations in other areas. The most frequently used aspect of this type of CRM analysis involves the predictive modelling of site location. This technique has been commonly used in areas where the management of the archaeological resource is restricted by either a poorly documented record, or limited information regarding the location of sites. This type of deductive approach is often centred on observed correlations between the distribution of archaeological material and a range of environmental factors such as slope, aspect, elevation and proximity (*cf.* Kuna and Adelsbergerová 1995). There have been a number of outlines (e.g. Marozas and Zack 1990, Warren 1990a) and case studies (e.g. Hasenstab and Resnick 1990, Warren 1990b) that have approached these issues in this way. Altchul (1990) offered a philosophical alternative when presenting a critique of this approach, arguing that such models were capable only of revealing what was already known. Instead he argued that an approach based upon 'red-flagging' was preferable. Rather than just providing 'accurate' distributions, extrapolating patterns of data already recognised, the GIS could be used to highlight (or 'red-flag') areas where increased archaeology may be encountered by a developer and where mitigation may be more costly. Further, he wished to expand the technique to highlight anomalies of significance, rather than merely showing patterns.

The basis for this type of modelling lies in the protection of the unknown archaeological resource through its statistical identification. The value of this technique is clear in relation to the activities of developers and the need for archaeological mitigation strategies. However, a number of more fundamental criticisms have arisen over this technique. Firstly, the results from it are essentially difficult to test without high expenditure, and so the results will lack robustness. Secondly, the prevailing requirement to model archaeological patterns in relation to environmental factors may be considered to be deterministic (see Gaffney and van Leusen 1995 for conflicting views). As such the technique remains as a large discipline in itself, with its own conflicting paradigms and discourse.

The third issue relating to CRM is management. This concerns archaeology as a known resource within the landscape, with its own considerations, but as one of many other landscape interests. Management issues typically involve financial and political decision-making in addition to directing research aims. Such approaches to GIS have been particularly prevalent within areas where wide-ranging interests, each with large datasets, lie together, such as within National Parks. For example, the GIS for Exmoor National Park consists of data covering archaeology and many other environmental themes. In relation to GIS, applications relating to management extend from basic data storage and display to more complex issues.

WHY THIS BOOK?

The aim of this book is to provide a background to the ways in which landscape archaeology problems, themes and questions may begin to be addressed by GIS. In contrast to many on the subject, the focus here is the principal issues regarding landscape archaeology in practice and the ways in which GIS can be used to address these issues and provide new approaches, new answers and new questions. Consequently, the following chapter begins with a consideration of the types of data currently being generated within the broad sphere of landscape archaeology. It also considers these pre-existing sources in relation to how GIS may be applied to what is being done currently, and also introduces some of the themes of GIS within the context of how they might be used in archaeology. This is followed in chapter 3 with a consideration of spatial data, addressing the definitions and themes of such data within landscape archaeology generally, and in relation to GIS applications particularly. In chapters 4 and 5, the methods of procuring data to input into the GIS is examined, including commercially available data, archives such as record offices and data gathered through field survey.

Chapters 6, 7 and 8 begin to consider the ways in which GIS can be used to address the questions and issues of landscape archaeology in the three areas of landscape analysis, reconstruction and theory respectively. In each chapter, the key themes of that area of landscape archaeology are considered and addressed through examples. Chapter 9 continues this theme, bringing the overall issues of interpretation together, considering how approaches combining each of these three landscape archaeology themes become possible within a GIS, and how this provides increased value to the archaeologist. This is followed in chapter 10 by a consideration of how these techniques and others may be used to address issues of archaeological landscape management. Chapter 11 considers the ways in which GIS may be used as an illustrative tool and how, through the visual reconstruction of past landscapes, new opportunities of interpretation and presentation are generated. The final chapter, chapter 12, brings the principal themes of the book together and offers some concluding remarks for those addressing landscape archaeology through the spatial sciences.

2

Landscape archaeology and data

INTRODUCTION

If the point of departure lies within landscape archaeology, the first theme to consider is what types of data are normally collected within the framework of 'landscape archaeology'. Furthermore, how might these data be fruitfully engaged with by using GIS? This chapter considers the ways in which GIS can be used to enrich the power of datasets already obtained within landscape archaeology. In later chapters, the ways in which GIS can address more specific issues within landscape archaeology will be considered.

Taking the definition in chapter 1 (Collins 1992), 'the unit of analysis is the artefact rather than the site'. In practice, landscape archaeology normally begins with the analysis of maps and other sources from record offices including aerial photography and records of previous work, followed by field methods such as fieldwalking and walkover surveys, in addition to earthwork and geophysical survey. The variability in data sources may be reflected in the variability in their spatial resolution, with data collected at a variety of scales. In this chapter, the different traditional sources of landscape archaeology data are considered in relation to the issues they each present with regards to GIS.

MAPS

Perhaps the first source of data used for projects involving a landscape archaeological element is the map. Maps can take many different forms and can display varying types of information at a variety of scales, survey accuracy and depiction. Normally, a modern map will provide information regarding basic location against which to plot sites and finds, in addition to providing information regarding topography. This includes the positions of watercourses and the shape of the landscape through the contours. Using just these very fundamental elements it is possible to begin to interpret site locations and to explore how sites relate to their local landscape. Furthermore, maps, normally those at 1:25,000 scale or higher, will provide a plan of field shapes which may provide morphological clues that may in turn both assist in identifying new sites and providing context to those sites that are already known.

In addition to modern maps, historical maps can be extremely valuable to landscape archaeologists (7). For example, in the UK the early Ordnance Survey mapping can be extremely useful for providing a picture of a landscape around the year 1900, depending on the area being studied. However, earlier maps, such as tithe maps and estate maps, can often push back the dating to much earlier, providing snapshots into the past that would not be possible in any other way. It is the combination of mapping evidence that is arguably of most use to the landscape archaeologist.

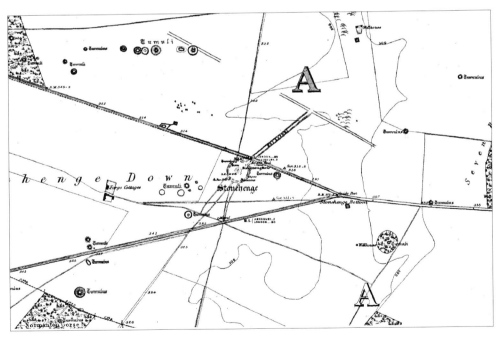

7 *Above:* Historical maps are fundamental to landscape archaeology, such as this nineteenth-century Ordnance Survey map of the Stonehenge area on Salisbury Plain, Wiltshire

8 *Opposite:* Aerial photograph – earthwork remains of Ellerton Priory, on the River Derwent south-east of York

RECORD OFFICES

A second resource commonly used by landscape archaeologists are the databases held by record offices. In the UK these include the Sites and Monuments Record (SMR) and Historic Environmental Record (HER) offices, the National Monuments Record (NMR) and other regional record offices. Commonly data are held either digitally or on index cards, though normally relating to sequential numbering on a map base. They provide information regarding previously discovered sites, normally for use within the planning process in advance of development, but of obvious value to landscape archaeologists.

AERIAL PHOTOGRAPHY

A method ubiquitous to the landscape archaeologist is aerial photography (*8*) and the identification of features from shadows, soil marks or crop marks

within the fields (Riley 1944, 1982, Wilson 1982). Aerial photography may be categorised into two principal types – vertical and oblique. Normally, though not exclusively, vertical photographs are used for activities such as mapping and are often printed at a given scale, whereas archaeological oblique photographs, also known as specialist photographs, are taken by an archaeologist whilst in flight using less sophisticated equipment.

Whilst numerous archives of both types of aerial photography exist within record offices and on the internet, their applicability within GIS requires some understanding. The formats of aerial photographs are normally as prints that may be digitised through scanning. Vertical photographs will not normally need much rectification, although lens distortion towards the edges of a photograph might warp the features. In the case of oblique photographs, rectification is always needed before they may be applied within a GIS. In both cases, but particularly in the case of oblique photographs, it is common for any archaeological feature to not be contained within a single print, but be spread across several prints. In many cases these features may have been transcribed, either by hand or digitally (see Wilson 1982 for more detail).

Readily available vertical photographs or transcriptions may be digitised through scanning to provide a raster image. In some cases such digital formats are available from national or regional bodies and record offices. Sometimes, though more rarely, transcribed features are available as digitised vector files consisting largely of lines. In these cases it may be possible to import the data directly into the GIS. With digitised raster photographs or transcriptions, data can be brought into the GIS for further analysis, comparison with other data formats, or digitisation into vectors.

Bringing a raster image, whether it is a vertical photograph or a transcription, requires a number of considerations. Firstly is resolution, or the number of pixels that represent the image, as this will influence the type of detail that may be digitised as vectors from it. Secondly is georeferencing – the process of placing the image in its correct location. In other words, cells within the image (pixels) need to be matched to geographical locations within the GIS. There are a number of ways of achieving this within the various GIS software packages, but the ultimate result is an image that fits in geographical space, thus with pixels that maintain a specific geographic size, dependent on the resolution of the original scanned image.

The advantages of transforming the results from aerial survey into a GIS environment are numerous. Firstly, it becomes possible to overlay these with other data, such as the point data generated from fieldwalking or walkover survey. Secondly, it becomes possible to consider the photograph or transcription in relation to other forms of data such as topography or geology, dependent on other layers that may be available within the GIS. This may be achieved through draping the raster images over DEMs of the topography. The georeferenced image also provides the basis for digitising lines, or vectors, relating to archaeological features. In the same way as for point data, these can be ascribed attributes within the database, perhaps according to type of feature, likely date and so forth.

Hence, within the GIS it becomes possible to overlay different types of data together to assess correlations between archaeological features identified on the photographs and any other natural or archaeological features. It also enables the creation of new data including interpretative transcriptions.

FIELD DATA

One of the earliest approaches to studying a landscape will be to walk over the area. The way this is approached may be determined by other data sources, such as previously known finds or perhaps features identified on aerial photographs. Both fieldwalking and walkover surveys can be conducted in a number of methods, though these are principally either systematic or non-systematic. In the case of systematic surveys, the landscape may be divided into a grid for walking, particularly in the case of fieldwalking (Gaffney *et al.* 1991), or fieldworkers will be required to walk across the landscape in transects set at specific intervals apart (e.g. Van de Noort and Ellis 1995). In contrast to this, and often the case within walkover surveys, assessment of the landscape may be more qualitative. In the case of pastoral upland landscapes, it might not be feasible to attempt any intense or systematic survey and so a more subjective approach is used.

Whatever the approach to fieldwalking or walkover surveys, the results commonly share the format of dots on maps, or a list of coordinates, each relating to the finding of an artefact or a site. In terms of GIS approaches, this is referred to as 'point data', and this will be covered in more detail later on. Point data at its simplest form consists of just a position that can be plotted within the GIS as a dot, perhaps against a map, though not necessarily. Additional information may be held for each point, such as type of find, date, material and so forth as a database or list.

Once input into a GIS, most simply as a list of data, it becomes possible to perform a number of display and analytical processes. At the most basic level it becomes possible to display the positions of the data points, perhaps in relation to other forms of data already held in the GIS, but again this will be covered later. Secondly, it becomes possible to interrogate the point data in order to identify groups. For example, the data may be examined and displayed in relation to date, type, material, or any other factor that is within the database or listing associated with each position (*9*).

9 Fieldwalking data represented in a GIS

More sophisticatedly, point data such as those from fieldwalking and walkover surveys may be examined in terms of clustering (*colour plate 1*). This can be achieved at a range of complexities in order to define groups. Owing to the nature of artefact survival, it is often easier in landscape archaeology to look to the bigger picture, and thus procedures such as density analysis become extremely useful. In chapter 1 the themes of vector and raster data structures were introduced. In this context, point data may be considered as vector data – just points in virtual space. A density model converts this vector data into a continuous raster format, or grid of 'cells' at a given resolution, perhaps each cell being 1 x 1m, 10 x 10m or 50 x 50m. In any case, each cell within the raster is the same size in spatial terms. Within the raster, each cell contains an attribute which may relate to any factor including elevation, colour, or number of artefacts. In converting the vector point data to a raster density plot, the computer determines a value for each cell based upon the density of point data. Whilst there are numerous parameters that may be adjusted in such an approach, ultimately the resulting model shows a raster with each cell value being equivalent to a value such as the number of finds per square kilometre.

The advantage of an application of density analysis to point data is that it may be used to generalise the data. The point data obtained from fieldwalking, for example, will be determined by a number of factors such as ploughing regime, depth of archaeological burial, damage to the archaeology and so on. Furthermore, often certain areas of the landscape might not currently be available for access to fieldwalkers, such as wooded coverts or built-on areas. In these cases it is important to obtain a more general picture of the data, highlighting the concentrations of data. Similarly it is important to identify whether there are patterns in the data, perhaps indicative of foci of activity, or whether artefacts are spread more generally, in the case of activities such as manuring perhaps.

Such generalisations of the data can be extremely useful with regards to making decisions over the management of resources when conducting future fieldwork. Following the principle of 'from the known to the unknown', the density plots provide a centre for activity that can form the starting points for later research that can then be extended into the wider landscape. However, whilst this method addresses some of the issues of non-systematic data recovery on the ground, it should always be considered that the more systematic a study, the better the results.

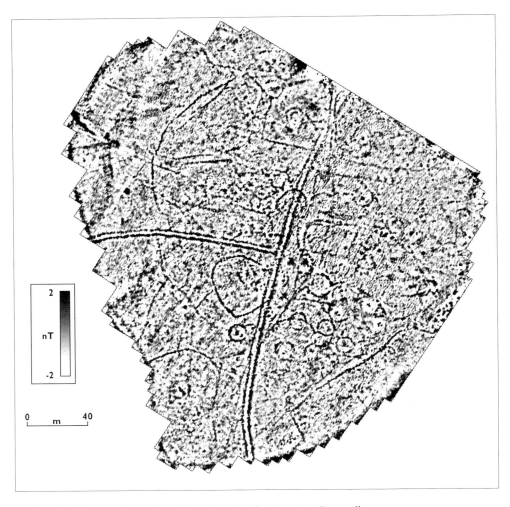

10 Geophysical raster data – Gear Farm Iron Age fort interior, Cornwall

GEOPHYSICAL SURVEY

As for aerial photographic data, the results from the variety of methods of geophysical survey are commonly output as raster images (*10*). In the same way as for aerial photography, these images can be georeferenced and transformed so that they occupy geographical space within the GIS. From here it becomes possible to correlate anomalies with other forms of data, or to drape the geophysical image over topography or any other surface. Furthermore, it is possible to digitise vector lines and polygons as interpretative layers, generating new data from the raster image.

Additionally, further functionality of GIS enables other analyses of geophysical data. As a raster, it becomes possible to perform image analyses to differentiate between trends in the data. Other formats of geophysical data might include x, y, z formats, where x and y provide a position in geographical space for each cell of the image, and z provides values, such as positive or negative nanotessla (nT). Using interpolation techniques it can be possible within the GIS to convert these data to different formats and to analyse them to highlight variations and subtleties, with the potential of identifying more subtle features.

CONCLUSIONS

This chapter has examined some of the data that are commonly collected in non-GIS led landscape archaeology. It has examined how these data may usefully be examined within a GIS environment, with the possible types of other approaches that may be used in order to obtain more information from the data. It has also provided an application-based introduction to GIS, and leading on from the introduction in the previous chapter, has identified some of the key themes. These include different types of raster and vector data structures, and concepts such as georeferencing and digitising. This leads us into chapter 3 where the nature of spatial data will be examined in more detail.

3
Spatial data

INTRODUCTION

Before considering the role of GIS within the various disciplines characterised by the term 'landscape archaeology' there should be some appreciation of the fundamentals of spatial data. Essentially, a GIS is a 'spatial database' which means that it is a database with the facility to store, manage and analyse data in terms of its position in the world, albeit in a virtual sense. This is where some element of discrepancy arises. The GIS only simulates the physical world and, in the case of archaeology, it can demonstrate how sometimes this simulation is the closest way of approaching the unknown, past realities being studied. This presents something of a problem as the simulation becomes the more important but its value is reliant on spatial data. Hence issues of spatial resolution and scale, the curvature of the earth, map projections and National Grids all provide the need for consideration and the possibility of error.

In this chapter the nature of spatial data is considered in relation to the history of mapping and the theoretical considerations of maps. The different ways of obtaining spatial data are also discussed with a view to the ways in which such data may be considered and prepared for use within the GIS.

WAYS OF CONSIDERING SPACE

At this juncture, it is profitable to consider different ways of conceptualising space and the mapping of the Earth's surface. Ethnographic evidence and the evidence from anthropology reveal other methods of mapping that are of importance to archaeology, at least at a conceptual level. The function of maps is of some significance here; essentially, why make a map in the first place? The principal reasons for creating maps may be categorised as for navigation, resource quantification, for strategic military reasons or for engineering.

11 Half-scale replica of one of the Bronze Age Ferriby Boats under sail. Navigation during prehistory is likely to have relied upon mental mapping of the relationship between waypoints

Navigation provides perhaps the most fundamental need for maps, but this has developed the most diverse cartographic responses (*11*). Navigation, or pathfinding, particularly through the translation of a route to a third party, is a concept that might take place on several levels. Essentially it is about waypoints that may be described and followed as a narrative. It has been argued that the history of navigation reflects a change from 'non-instrumental' (Needham 1971), also referred to as 'environmental' (McGrail 1987) in earlier periods, relating to pre-compass methods. Such approaches to navigation relied upon the identification of morphological characteristics that might be seen or otherwise experienced during passage. 'Mental mapping' is a concept that has been used to explain how this process of navigation without physical maps might have worked in practice, with pathfinding achieved through the creation of a dynamic, changing and continually updated mental image of waypoints (Oakley 1977). Gell (1985) has further demonstrated how much of this process would have relied upon a level of 'practical logic', providing structure to Bourdieu's (1977) concept of 'practical mastery' of the route, involving personal experience before a route could be known and subjected to the 'mental map'.

'Quantitative navigation' is the name given to approaches to wayfinding that use instruments, such as the compass, as a way of measuring space. It is at this stage of navigational history that cartography began to become established in Europe. For example, the creation of Mercator's Projection of the Earth's surface onto a flat chart (see below) was undertaken to ensure that shipping routes could be accurately mapped. This process of navigation relates to the use of other measurements too, including stellar observation and the measurement of distance 'over ground'. According to Needham (1971) 'quantitative navigation' was supplanted by 'mathematical navigation'. The latter process related to a higher level of mapping calculation and it is within this system that the fundamentals of GPS navigation and GIS themselves lie.

The second principal motivation for map-making may be classified as 'resource quantification'. The vast majority of early maps were created in order to address issues such as taxation. The tithe maps in the United Kingdom, for example, were drawn up in order to calculate acreage of land so that people could be taxed appropriately for funding the parish clergy. This method was so important that legislation in 1831 established Tithe Districts. Similarly, estate maps were usually drawn up to serve a quantification exercise, either related to taxation or for general management purposes.

The third motivation for the creation of maps lies with military tactics and strategy. The origins of the Ordnance Survey lie in the need to generate maps of areas where potential uprisings might have occurred in order to be used for strategic purposes (see below for a full discussion of the Ordnance Survey).

Finally, maps may be generated for engineering purposes. Indeed, many of the decisions relating to the scales used on Ordnance Survey mapping reflected the requirements of the engineers of the Industrial Revolution, and particularly the building of railways (see below). Ultimately, in these cases a quantification of the landscape is undertaken in order to calculate where to build, the quantity of raw materials required and so forth.

Essentially, therefore, the ontogeny of mapping, particularly in the Cartesian sense (as viewed from above), extends back over several centuries in order to fulfil a range of requirements. These requirements have influenced the types of maps created, including their scales and their projections. It is within this trajectory that GIS has come into existence.

SPACE AND LANDSCAPE ARCHAEOLOGY

The role of space within landscape archaeology would at first appear to be very obvious. Landscape, by definition, would involve space. However, within archaeology there have been a number of different approaches to the consideration of space, borrowing on a range of broader academic disciplines. Fundamentally the consideration of space from the perspective of landscape archaeology can be divided between practical and theoretical approaches.

Practical approaches to landscape archaeology have been focused on the identification of archaeological sites (e.g. Ordnance Survey 1973, Wood 1963, Wilson 1982), distribution maps and the interpretation of sequencing and phasing within the landscape (e.g. Hoskins 1955, Aston 1985, Muir 2000). In addition to physically identifying sites, either through remains visible on the ground or through aerial photography, the approach has been to identify diagnostic patterns within the existing landscape that provide clues to the past landscape. By incorporating other sources including place names, historical documents and cartographic material, it can be possible to build up a picture of how the landscape has physically changed through time, in conjunction with a pragmatic consideration of potentially influential factors such as watercourses and topography. In addition to these approaches, other considerations of the landscape have been made through the investigation of palaeoenvironmental factors.

Theoretical interpretations of space consider it to be a cultural construct. In other words, distinction is made between particular locations of activity (places) and areas between them (spaces – *cf.*Tuan 1977). Furthermore, consideration of space (and/or places) has been influenced by the recognition that landscape has cultural meaning that falls outside the limits of pragmatic interpretation. To take a modern example, council planning policy guidance will influence where new settlements may be built probably more so than considerations of the physical features of the area. In the past cultural considerations will have manifest meaning and symbolism in the landscape that will have influenced how and where different activities might have taken place. One key text that began to examine these theories in relation to landscape archaeology specifically was *A phenomenology of landscape* by Christopher Tilley (1994) which examined the interplay between *places* and *spaces*, and the role of the individual as a vehicle for experiencing the landscape. He and others have subsequently argued that many traditional approaches to landscape archaeology, including distribution maps and site plans, are of limited value since past landscapes were about the people and how they viewed their world. Instead there has been a greater emphasis on the 'embodied' landscape, assessing factors such as intervisibility between monuments and the experience of moving through the landscape.

These various considerations of space from the perspective of landscape archaeology provide something of a problem for the landscape archaeologist wishing to take a more holistic view. In addition to these themes, the advent of GIS-based approaches has resulted in an increased interest in quantitative approaches to understanding landscape archaeology.

PRINCIPLES OF SPATIAL DATA

Fundamentally, spatial data refer to any information that has a location component. It is abstract insofar as it simulates chosen elements of the real world, whilst remaining 'virtual'. Certain features may be recorded, such as trench positions or archaeological features, whilst others might not be recorded, including perhaps modern or temporary structures. Furthermore, certain features might be recorded at a very high resolution, such as the positions of small finds within an excavation trench, whereas other features might demand a lower level of accuracy, such as the recording of wide banks.

All maps, whether paper or digital (as in the case of GIS), represent the elements of the real world using some type of two- or three-dimensional approach. The two-dimensional approach, based on X and Y, refer to the 'plan' of the ground, in other words representing it as a flat image as if seen from above. The third dimension, Z, refers to elevation or height, and may be expressed as contours, spot heights or modelled three-dimensionally.

The principal two dimensions that represent the world from above, or in plan, are variously labelled as longitude and latitude, X and Y or Eastings and Northings. Effectively they each place a grid over the world so that the positions of all features can be expressed in terms of either angles or distances. For each type of grid, positions are related to a datum or starting point. Hence positions are measured as so far east of this point, and so far north. In the case of National Grids the datum point or origin is normally a point towards the south-west corner of the area being mapped, from which positions are measured in both directions. Spherical grids, such as longitude and latitude, measure these distances in terms of degrees of arc, again starting from a given datum point, such as the equator for latitude and Greenwich for longitude. Angular measurements reflect the spherical shape of the planet; whereas distances from the datum consider the world to be at least locally flat (see below).

For the purposes of most mapping, and particularly within the GIS environment, grids expressed in terms of distances from the datum are the normal method of defining position. Commonly, these expressions are given in relation to a National Grid (see below) that provides a position relative to grid north, although local grids can also be used, with an arbitrary datum point, normally expressed as 0-East and 0-North, or 100-East and 200-North, and so on, so that a find that is 1m to both the north and east of this datum may be at 101-East and 201-North.

PROJECTIONS AND NATIONAL GRIDS

From as early as the sixth century BC and the work of Pythagoras it has been understood that the Earth is not flat. This fact has provided cartographers with a number of challenges. Owing to the fact that the Earth is *broadly* spherical, and that maps are generally flat representations of its surface, some kind of error may be assumed from the translation from one form to the other (*12*).

Approaches to mapping have centred on what is known as projections. In cartography, a projection is the means of depicting the spherical surface of the earth on a flat piece of paper – essentially how a curved surface is translated to the flat map. Flemish cartographer Gerardus Mercator developed a projection in the sixteenth century that enabled the course of a ship steering on a constant bearing to be represented as a straight line on the map. This projection is still in use today and has formed the basis of many National Grid systems. However, whatever method is used there will be some level of error for larger areas and this will relate directly to the distances being covered. Historically some of this error was discarded within areas of the landscape that were considered to be less likely to be measured, such as river valleys or areas of moorland, by effectively cutting out parts of the measured map to fit the grid (see below).

Different GIS packages approach the subject of projection in different ways, with some developing methods of transposing between different projection systems. Within archaeological studies two factors – how big the site is, and your whereabouts – often determine the choice of projection. If your site is very small it is possible to work accurately to a local grid that might be tied to a National Grid. Where sites are bigger or where whole landscapes are being studied, perhaps at the county scale, then considerations of projection become important. Measurements between places within a National Grid might be different from those on the ground due to the nature of the projection. Your whereabouts becomes important for a number of reasons. Many larger countries have several National Grids to counter the problems of error caused by projections. In these cases the appropriate projection and grid will need to be sought.

ELEVATION

Expressing the third dimension on a two-dimensional map requires some element of depiction. Traditionally the mapping of height has been achieved through spot heights marked on the map, or by using contours (*13*). Contours as a method of depicting areas of shared elevation value were famously invented by the mathematician Charles Hutton in 1774. This was really more of a by-product

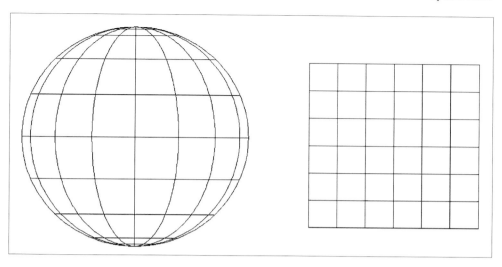

12 Comparison of spherical and normal grids demonstrating the need for projections

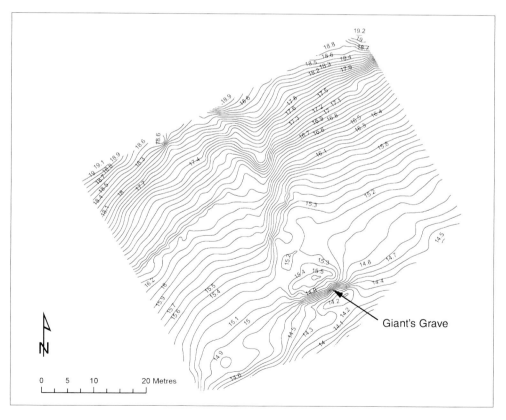

13 Using contours to represent elevation – Giant's Grave Viking burial, Fetlar, Shetland

from a broader attempt to calculate the mass of the Earth by measuring the mass of Schiehallion Mountain in Scotland to assess the relative gravitational pull of both. The contouring became a means to make some sense of the numerous spot heights across the mountain generated by the team of surveyors for the purpose. Essentially contours are lines of equal elevation that enable factors such as slope and topographic shape to be visualised. Thus, where lines depicting equal vertical intervals are closer together it is indicative of a steeper slope and where they are further apart the represented landscape is flatter.

The issues relating to the depiction of elevation come from a number of standpoints. From the perspective of map projections, relative changes in elevation over considerable distances will result in loss of accuracy as the spherical Earth effectively drops away. This needs to be accounted for. Furthermore, and as with all cartographic representation, the accuracy of the height depiction is limited by the survey data. Normally only a certain resolution of measurements will be recorded with the areas between the points being estimated, or interpolated. Mapping height is achieved through a number of diverse methods, including ground survey, using a variety of instruments, from aerial photography and the use of photogrammetry, and more recently through the use of other remote LIght sensing techniques such as LIDAR (LIght Detection And Ranging).

Different GIS software packages address elevation in a number of ways. Some packages do not deal with height in a three-dimensional way whilst others require additional software extension packages to be purchased in addition to the basic two-dimensional software. More generally, elevation can be addressed through graphical means, such as a scanned georeferenced image of contours, through the basic labelling of features (such as *XY* coordinates with an attached label representing its elevation) or, more sophisticatedly, through three-dimensional representation of surfaces. Two principal methods of three-dimensional representation are possible although in each case it should be noted that the third dimension is not 'real'. In other words the GIS provides a two-dimensional plot of *XY* coordinates in virtual space, with the additional *Z* coordinate represented as an attribute of the *XY* position. This is normally referred to as 2.5D as opposed to true 3D.

The two ways of representing elevation as a continuous surface within a GIS are as a grid or as a TIN. A grid is a representation of a surface that divides the landscape into equal square blocks. Each of these blocks has an attribute that relates to its elevation. For example, an area being studied might cover 5 x 5km, and it might be decided that an appropriate resolution for a three-dimensional model is 10m, hence the landscape is divided into blocks each measuring 10 x 10m (500 x 500 blocks for the whole landscape). Each of your blocks, or cells, will have an individual attribute relating to its elevation. The second method, the TIN, is an acronym for Triangular Irregular Network. This is part of a broader mathematical concept of Polyhedral Irregular Networks, but focusing on triangles. A TIN is a network of triangular planes that join XYZ coordinates together. Hence, the input data might be a spread of XY coordinates each with a height value, Z. The TIN will be created so that triangles join between all the points, with smaller triangles being created between points that are closer together. Each of the resulting triangles will be a flat plane angled to join each of the three input points at their attributed heights.

SCALE AND RESOLUTION

A map is an abstract representation of the real world for a given purpose. Consequently, certain elements of the real world will be shown using representative symbols. Furthermore, features will be depicted at scale. Scale is denoted using a ratio figure, such as 1:10,000, which means that 1m on the map represents 10km on the ground. At a more useful level, 1cm on the map will represent 10,000cm, or 100m, on the ground.

Traditionally, cartography is undertaken at a pre-determined scale, and this will be determined by the requirements of the final product – the map (*14*). For urban areas, mapping will normally need to provide greater detail than an area of open fields. For example, the highest resolution commercial mapping in the UK is at a scale of 1:1250, though this is only available for built-up areas, with many rural areas not being surveyed at any scale greater than 1:2500.

Archaeological survey, as demonstrated by the work conducted traditionally by the Royal Commission on the Historical Monuments, and now partially undertaken by English Heritage, came from a background in the Ordnance Survey. Hence, the methods used for depicting archaeological features such as earthworks follow those used for more traditional mapping requirements. Earthwork remains are surveyed at a given scale, which may range perhaps between 1:2500 to 1:100, depending on the needs of the survey. High-resolution analytical survey, aimed at interpreting phasing and so forth, will clearly provide a very different result compared with a lower resolution survey. The cartographic product is therefore at a scale which remains static and so the scales cannot be used interchangeably; a low-resolution survey should not be used for a higher resolution study, for example.

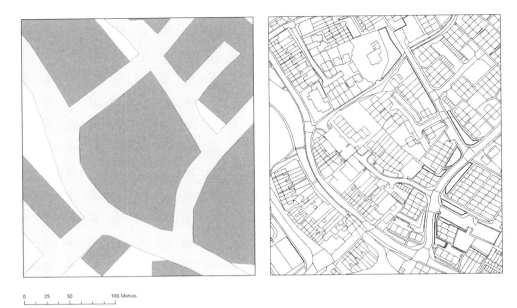

14 How the same features may be depicted within different resolution mapping. The image on the left shows an urban area mapped at 1:50,000 scale, whilst the image on the right shows the same area at 1:1000

THE ORDNANCE SURVEY — A CASE STUDY IN CARTOGRAPHIC HISTORY

The nature of scale is fundamental to issues of cartography, and one that provides crucial context for all mapping. So far it has been established that maps are representations of the real world made to fit a particular purpose and that scale choice is essential in fulfilling this purpose. The case of the Ordnance Survey demonstrates the issues relating to scale.

The need for accurate mapping was realised during the eighteenth century when George II was at war with France, but also faced Scottish rebellion. For strategic reasons, he commissioned a survey of the Scottish highlands in 1746, which was undertaken by William Roy. This began the process of mapping, which was continued for the south coast by the end of that same century due to fear of revolution.

Gradually additional areas were mapped, with the first map being published in 1801 — a 1in to the mile scale depiction of the county of Kent. By 1820 maps at this scale covered approximately a third of England and Wales, but by 1824 a new scale of 6in to the mile was developed with the commissioning of mapping

Ireland. This new scale began to increase in importance due to changes in the tithe mapping of the country and the setting up of 'Tithe Districts'. Additional pressure on the requirement for higher resolution mapping came with the boom in railway construction. Fundamentally, the original 1in to the mile scale maps were too generalising to be of use to the engineers constructing the railways and, furthermore, the 1in series hadn't been completed. The need for accurate mapping lead to the development of rights for surveyors to access all areas for the purposes of cartography in 1841.

Following the fire at the Tower of London in 1841 and the subsequent movement of the Ordnance Survey offices to Southampton, further decisions needed to be made relating to scales for mapping. In 1863, final decisions were made. The resulting choices lead to the mapping of moorland or mountainous areas at a scale of 6in to the mile (1:10,560), the mapping of rural areas at a scale of 25in to the mile, and urban areas at 10in to the mile. The 1in series (1:63,360) was also retained. By 1895 the first mapping of the whole country at 25in to the mile scale was completed, known as the First Edition County Series. An updated mapping at the same scale followed this, known as the Second Edition.

Up to the 1930s mapping had been covered on a county by county basis; hence, the 25in County Series First and Second Editions. However, by this time, choices relating to national mapping were being considered. One of the problems had been that the County Series mapping had assumed a flat surface of the Earth. They were extremely accurate but if edges of two county maps were matched together then problems began to arise. Essentially the errors generated by the translation of the spherical surface of the planet to a flat map began to be apparent when considering such large areas. In order to address this issue, and to begin to develop a national mapping strategy, 1935 saw the re-triangulation of Britain and the establishment of the National Grid; which is still used today.

The National Grid for the United Kingdom uses a Transverse Mercator Projection to counter the issues of flat mapping and the pushing of map error caused by the spherical surface to areas such as moorland. The system uses Eastings and Northings to calculate position in a consistent coordinate system and the resulting series of maps follow scales that fit within this system.

SPACE AND GIS

So far the nature of space in its three dimensions and in relation to different coordinate systems and map projections has been considered. Within a GIS space is understood in two principal ways from the basis of the two data formats: vector and raster.

Vector data aim to represent features in a way that is as close to the original as possible or appropriate (Burrough 1986). Vectors may be considered as principally points, lines or polygons (*15*).

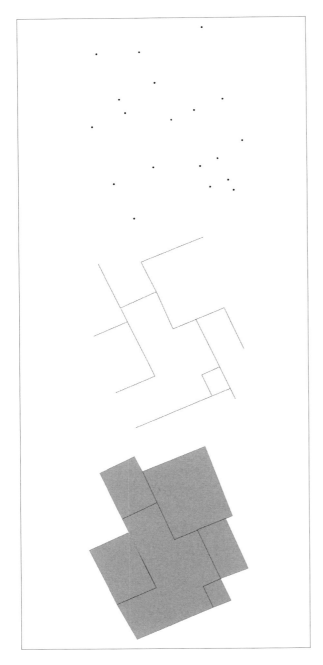

15 Different types of vector data – points, lines and polygons

A point will represent a position in space defined by a coordinate. A line connects a series of 'nodes'. A polygon defines area and may be used to define topology; the relationships between different areas. The vector data may be attached to a database providing the potential for multiple attributes to be stored in relation to the spatial unit. For example, a point file within an archaeological record, such as the SMR, might contain information regarding the name of site, its period, size, type of remains, county, original finder, any published information and so forth. Thus is becomes possible to use the GIS to formulate an enquiry and display all sites of a certain period, for example. Furthermore, it becomes possible to interrogate the database in numerous ways in order to examine the data spatially. Vector data relies on topological relationships between different features, particularly in the case of polygon layers. For example, a polygon representation of a geology map should be constructed of polygons for each of the geology types, with no gaps between them, and no overlaps. Thus, anywhere within the layer, the geological type may be identified. From this, it becomes possible to interrogate other vector data. Following the example of the geological map, it might be useful to understand what proportion of wetland sites lie within alluvial deposits compared to peatlands. A simple spatial interrogation of a point file containing an attribute for wetland sites may be spatially compared with the geology map to provide numbers of sites in each area.

The alternative to vector data structures is the raster. Simply, a raster consists of an array of grid cells, also referred to as pixels (*16*). Each cell within the grid is referenced in relation to the row and column upon which it is situated, providing its location, with an attribute providing a value.

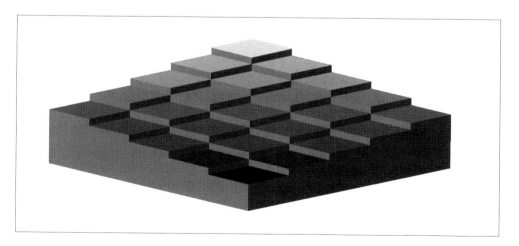

16 Representing elevation within a raster dataset. Each cell covers a standard area and represents values according to height

This value may relate to a colour, as in the case of photographs or maps, or might relate to elevation, as in the case of terrain models. In georeferenced rasters, each cell is generated at a given size on the ground providing the raster resolution. For example, each cell may relate to 10 x 10m and so the attribute value for that cell covers this whole parcel of land. Unlike vector data, with rasters only one attribute may be held by each cell. Higher resolution rasters (i.e. smaller cells) will result in potentially greater detail, with each cell representing a smaller land parcel. However, increased resolution has implications in terms of storage space. In the case of images such as aerial photographs, scanned maps or the results from geophysical survey, the image will need to be georeferenced before it is useable within the GIS. This procedure normally occurs within the GIS, whereby identifiable positions on the image are provided with real–world coordinates. This can be achieved in a number of ways, which include the generation of an attached table of coordinates for the corners of the image, or through directly clicking on the image, perhaps on a junction of field boundaries, and either entering the projected coordinates directly or else dragging the image to the correct position against another mapping layer. Once the image has been georeferenced it becomes possible to interrogate as with a raster that might display other values such as elevation.

A third data structure available within GIS is the Triangular Irregular Network, or TIN (Peuker *et al.* 1978), also referred to occasionally as Polyhedral Irregular Networks. A TIN is a vector-based topological structure that creates surfaces normally of elevation that uses sheets of continuous, connected triangular facets based upon Delaunay triangulation of irregularly spaced data which form the points of the triangles. The advantages of a TIN data format lie in its ability to model directly from the data, particularly maintaining lines such as stream beds. The raster alternative relies on interpolation that may generate computational artefacts between input–data points which might lead to peaks and troughs within what should be a flat surface. Fundamentally, a TIN is a vector-based topological structure.

Once data are processed in any of the GIS formats different layers can be presented, examined and analysed together. Vectors may be displayed overlying rasters or TINs and may form the basis for interrogating them. The limitations of rasters to hold a single attribute for each cell means that overlaying different rasters with different information becomes important. If each raster overlies the same Cartesian area and has the same cell size, then it is possible to examine different attributes for the same area. This might be comparing elevation from a terrain raster with other rasters perhaps displaying slope or aspect and so forth.

The relative usefulness of different types of GIS data structures are considered in more detail in chapter 5, with reference to methods of generating models of landscape, and the efficacy of the various interpolation techniques.

CONCLUSIONS

In this chapter the nature of spatial data has been examined, including the ways in which it may be considered in maps, and ultimately why maps have been made. The ways in which space is understood or socially constructed have been outlined, and how this process can impact on the way that space may have been viewed in the past and how it is viewed in the present has been discussed. Furthermore, the principles of spatial data have been considered, particularly in relation to themes of map projections, elevation, scale and resolution. Much of this is evident in the case study of the Ordnance Survey.

At this juncture, and for the purposes of GIS, space may be considered as a series of geographical positions that may be understood through coordinates to give position and attributes such as elevation to provide additional detail. This is fundamental to the nature of GIS which considers any area as a grid within which layers are plotted. Hence the x and y coordinates remain as a constant against which attributes are measured, depicted and analysed. The following chapter examines the ways in which data may be obtained for input within a GIS environment.

4

Procuring data

INTRODUCTION

To be functional, GIS requires data. One advantage of GIS is that it can generate new data from existing data, but it does require these data in the first place. In chapter 2 some of the types of landscape data were considered in terms of how they might be better used within a GIS, as a way of introducing the functionality of the software. Chapter 3 considered this further in relation to the nature of spatial data in relation to GIS. This chapter further considers data for use within the GIS, focusing on different types of data, including archaeological, cartographic and survey data, all of which may be used together within a single system. This is considered in conjunction with the themes outlined in the previous chapter such as spatial resolution, scale and depiction.

Archaeological data encompasses an extremely broad range of different types obtained from a number of different sources, and this is outlined in part in the previous chapter. Principally, archaeological data may reflect the positions of sites or finds, in addition to transcriptions of site plans or features identified on aerial photographs. The sources for these data include a range of books and articles, in addition to archives held by museums and record offices. Often the nature of the data will determine where it is held, although the first avenue of investigation will normally be with regional or national archaeological data repositories. In the UK, these include the National Monuments Record (NMR) held by English Heritage in their offices in Swindon, and the various Sites and Monuments Records (SMR) and Historic Environment Records (HER) held regionally. In addition, other sources of data might be from agencies and commercial units.

In terms of integrating archaeological data within the GIS, much of the information available to archaeologists is provided in image format, such as geophysical plots, aerial photographs, surveys and so forth. Integration of these rasters within the GIS requires a process of georeferencing whereby the image is rectified so that it lies within the appropriate coordinate space, such that distances can be measured from the image, and coordinates of locations on the image can be outputted. This section explores the different types of archaeological data that are available and indicates how they might be profitably integrated within the GIS in terms of basic data input. However, it should always be considered that the value of the resulting GIS database is only as good as the data input into it, and this includes the resolution of the original images, the scanning resolution and the accuracy of georeferencing, which might rely on both the person performing the task, and the availability of identifiable positions that can be used to supply coordinates to the image, thereby georeferencing it.

The principal types of data relating to landscape archaeology are outlined in chapter 2. This chapter examines the ways in which these data sources may be integrated within GIS. It also covers the ways in which input data may be processed to generate new data, such as surfaces for contextualising and analysing landscapes.

MAPS

Mapping provides a basis for all GIS work and is fundamental to it. Normally some level of commercial mapping data will be required for any GIS project or database. At a basic level, mapping provides the coordinate system and scaling for integrating all other spatially referenced data. Cartographic data include a range of different types of material in various formats, and with the potential for converting data between formats, principally between raster and vector. As with any other data, different types of mapping will have their own levels of accuracy and there are issues regarding this. These issues are:

1. The intentionality of the map regarding its accuracy. Maps are normally generated for a particular task. Tithe maps were generated for economic purposes for calculating the taxable areas of land, as were many estate maps which also had purposes in planning further developments such as gardens or construction works. The intentions of the map maker might not always be identifiable, although some consideration of the possibilities will have implications for the accuracy of the original survey and hence the map, and what is actually depicted.

2. The surveying accuracy of the map. As mentioned in part above, different maps will have required differing levels of surveying accuracy. The most obvious example of this is the different scales of maps. Within a GIS, you have the potential ability for unlimited 'zooming in'. Clearly, obtaining pinpoint positions from a

map that was originally surveyed at a much lower scale would be inappropriate. This should always be considered when using maps in GIS, and in turn leads to the importance of maintaining metadata to ensure that any data derived from mapping layers makes a note of the original survey scale of the parent map.

3. The quality of georeferencing. As with other types of georeferenced raster, positions and measurements taken from the image within the GIS rely completely on the accuracy of the original georeferencing. This will be influenced by user error, as well as by the availability of identifiable positions on the image or map, that may be compared with known positions on your base map. Alternatively they might be georeferenced relative to GPS or other survey positions. Again, this will influence the accuracy of the resulting georeferenced image.

4. A further issue relates to the reissue of some historical mapping. In chapter 3, the integration of the National Grid by the Ordnance Survey was provided as an example of how mapping errors could occur when generating large areas of mapping on a flat projection. In some cases, commercially available historical mapping is provided with National Grid superimposed over it. Whilst this becomes a useful tool for providing general position, the original errors in integrating a County Series-based mapping to a National mapping system mean that the grid can often be inaccurate. Thus it is worth considering that, in most cases, it is most appropriate to georeference from identifiable features depicted on the map rather than to use the superimposed grid. At least, each case should be considered fully before proceeding with integrating data within the GIS.

5. Finally, the quality of digitising will impact on accuracy, as well as how the landscape features are digitised as vectors. Fundamentally, the care with which the digitising has been done will be important, but only in the context of the accuracy of the original raster map and its georeferencing, both mentioned above. However, additional factors that influence the usefulness of the final mapping layer lead from the nature of digitising, such as the use of different types of data structure, such as polygons, points or lines, for different features. The decisions made in how to depict certain features also influence the usefulness of the resulting product. Ultimately, any vector data will be derived from another source. Whilst this will often not be possible, where it is, it is useful to obtain the original data to check how the derivation took place.

Modern mapping

Modern mapping is available at a variety of resolutions and qualities depending upon the region in which you are working. Particularly, in some areas of some countries there is little or no recent mapping of features, requiring new data to be obtained. In the UK, current mapping is constantly being updated and can be purchased in a number of different formats and at a number of different scales, as either raster or vector formats. Commonly the vector formats are generated from an amalgam of maps, potentially of different scales, so that different parts of any one map tile might be more accurate than others. This information is normally invisible once the data is in the GIS. Whilst such issues should be remembered, it is normal for such vector-based data to be digitised from the most accurate maps available for any single area. Within the UK the introduction of MasterMap has produced a topologically correct polygon-based coverage which has revolutionised the potential of GIS.

Modern mapping, as mentioned previously, is of fundamental importance to the landscape archaeologist. Mapping can be incorporated within the GIS directly from commercially available data or, dependent upon copyright issues, can be obtained through scanning hard copies of maps and integrating them within the GIS through georeferencing.

Historical mapping

Historical mapping covers a range of different types of maps, at different qualities and different resolutions. In some cases, historical maps cannot be expected to provide more than a schematic understanding of space, such as the famous Inclesmoor map from the southern edge of the Humber. However, with more appropriately surveyed mapping, historical maps can be profitably utilised within the GIS environment. In the UK the principal historical maps relating to the nineteenth and early twentieth century are the first and second edition Ordnance Survey County Series maps (see chapter 3). These maps were generated at 1:2500 scale, and were conducted on a county by county basis. These maps predate the establishment of a National Grid and were thus not generated using a projection. As a result of this, the edges between counties rarely match correctly, although locally they are accurate. Hence, it is more appropriate to georeference a map for a particular area relative to local detail rather than the overlying National Grid.

The direct advantages of importing historical mapping into a GIS are numerous. Firstly, it may be possible to discredit certain features that might be visible on the ground as being the remnants of earlier datable field boundaries or buildings. Secondly, it is possible to begin to phase detail within the landscape, such as identifying landscape features that were created at a point between two different edition maps – for example, a field pattern that exists on a late nineteenth-century map where open fields were depicted on a map 50 years earlier. Thirdly, it becomes possible to identify oddities within the landscape pattern that might indicate either diagnostic features or else point to areas of interest. For example, a bend in a field boundary might indicate the presence of an earlier feature that no longer exists, such as a barrow. Fourthly, through the comparison of numerous historical maps it becomes possible to identify the position of an earlier feature. For example, George III's White House at Kew Gardens, London, demolished in 1802, is only identified on one eighteenth-century plan by William Chambers. There are no identifiable features on this plan that relate to the modern landscape, due to the subsequent wider landscaping of the area. However, through the use of georeferencing intermediate mapping together, it was possible to regress the mapping back so that the modern mapping could be compared with the original mapping of the White House. Hence it was possible to begin setting out the positions of the buildings on the ground. However, as mentioned above, any use of mapping, particularly historical mapping, will bring levels of error, some of which are un–quantifiable (see above).

Topographical data

The word 'topography' is a broad term referring to all natural and artificial features within a district. However, for the purposes of GIS, and specifically this book, I use the term to refer to data regarding the lie of the land; in other words, data about the shape of the land, particularly in three dimensions. Many archaeological projects will require a three-dimensional approach to landscape. The landscape may be constructed as a computer model that will both represent it, and provide the possibility for its analysis.

Topographical data may be acquired at a variety of resolutions, either available commercially, or through survey work (see below). The resolution of the topographical data will influence the types of analyses that may be performed on a surface and the reliability of the results stemming from them. Data is available in a number of formats, although these may normally be considered as either contour data or point data of some sort. Contour data consist of a file of polylines, each containing a height attribute. The density of these lines is measured by the interval between them; i.e. 1m contours compared to 10m contours. However, there is a tendency to consider contour data, of say 10m, to be of equal value. If you consider the nature of different landscapes, clearly there will be denser contour data for a hilly or mountainous landscape compared with a flood plain. Thus the usefulness of the contour data in terms of its resolution is very much dependent on the nature of the terrain that is to be modelled.

Point data, on the other hand, normally consists of points with height attributes at a given resolution. For example, this resolution might be a point every 10m or a point every 50m. Again, whilst the 10m resolution data will contain more information, it should be remembered that most of these datasets were derived from the same data as the contours, if not from the contours themselves, leading us to the same issue whereby there is generally less data for flatter areas than for topographically variable or hilly areas. Thus, different types of data are not so directly comparable. The creation of three-dimensional surfaces from topographical data is dealt with later in the following chapter.

Remote sensing data for mapping

Remote sensing data refers to those data that may be collected remotely and commonly involving the use of low-flying aircraft-based technologies that use optical or near infra-red wavelengths (*colour plate 2*). Since the 1970s remote sensing approaches have included the use of digital multispectral imaging sensors, thermal imaging radiometers and imaging RADAR. These approaches produce data that may be enhanced, rectified and reclassified using software to isolate and identify particular features within the landscape (Bewley *et al.* 1999). This type of data is available internationally over the internet from providers such as Intermap (www.intermap.com) and provides a solution to the problems identified with the resolution of input data. Using these data, available to 5m surface resolution, it is possible to model even relatively flat landscapes accurately due to the high resolution of data input. Increasingly common within archaeology is the use of LIDAR data, which can produce very high-resolution maps of topography able to identify subtle variations created by earthworks and other features. In addition to airborne remote sensing techniques, the use of satellite imagery using a number of different wavelengths and at various land-surface resolutions has become possible, although its use within archaeology remains limited.

The advantages of remote sensing data lie in the ability to collect data for large areas relatively rapidly and in the ability to identify subsurface features. For example, airborne thermal imagery, or Infrared Line Scanning technology, used mainly by the military can also be useful for detecting archaeology, although this, like aerial photography, is dependent upon flying at the correct time of day and within the correct environmental conditions. The use of LIDAR data has become more reliable in recent years due to the use of different bandwidths to effectively see below vegetation and trees. However, the problems with any undifferentiated system of data collection is that the data contain arguably too much modern detail, including buildings and cars, that may detract from the more subtle archaeological features. However, its application remains in its infancy and as such provides another reliable layer of data for integrating within GIS landscape models.

RECORD OFFICE DATA

In the case of each data repository, different types of recording and storage will have been undertaken which will reflect directly on how accessible data is for integration within a GIS project. For example, paper records will need to be digitised and digital records might need to be standardised into correct formats (see databases below). In many cases, archaeological data held within repositories is stored within GIS and may be directly available for use, although different GIS packages store data in different ways and so data might require conversion.

AERIAL PHOTOGRAPHY

A common tool within landscape archaeology is the use of aerial photography (see chapter 2). The use of aerial photography within a GIS environment may be in raster or vector format, the former relating to the integration of georeferenced images, as with geophysical plots and survey plans, the latter relating to the interpreted plot that might be available or generated as a vector layer. However, the potential for integrating aerial photography within GIS is dependent upon the nature of the aerial photograph. Principally, aerial photographs are either oblique or vertical. The former normally relate to specialist photography taken by archaeologists of features that have been identified and need to be recorded. The problem with oblique photographs is that they require some type of rectification, normally in another software package than GIS, to make them effectively vertical so that they can be added as a layer. The second type of aerial photograph is vertical, which is often non-specialist. Whilst a vertical photograph is much easier to georeference within the GIS, it will normally contain less information than a specialist oblique photograph. Furthermore, it is possible for lens distortion to occur towards the edges of any photographic image which should be considered prior to taking measurements from any photography.

FIELD DATA

Other types of data that might result from archaeological landscape-based fieldwork include surveyed plans of sites, as with either contour surveys or hatchured surveys (see Bowden 1999). For the time being these may be considered as plans that may be integrated into the GIS as images, or rasters, for storage and presentation against other layers of data. In this case, the GIS works as a map-overlay tool, much as many graphics packages can work, but with the added advantage of providing scaling and coordinates.

Additional archaeological data that might relate to a landscape archaeology GIS include gathered field data, either generated from GPS positions or from sketched or triangulated positions on maps. These positions might relate to the position of a monument in the landscape, or a find scatter derived from fieldwalking, for example. Inputting these data into the GIS is achieved in one of two ways. The first way is for the paper map containing all the data to be scanned, georeferenced and for the positions of sites to be digitised from the image. The second, perhaps more practical way, is to type the coordinates into a database, spreadsheet or word processing package, with a column providing information relating to each site. This can then be saved and uploaded into the GIS to provide point data for each of the sites.

GEOPHYSICAL DATA

Geophysical data may be incorporated within a GIS in a number of ways. The nature of geophysical data can take different forms depending on the method being used and the software processing the data (see chapter 2). Normally, however, the results from geophysical survey are either in the form of an image (greyscale or colour), or as an interpreted plot. Alternative outputs can be digitised, interpreted plots that might be imported as vector layers, or as digital data files. In the case of images, plans can be imported into the GIS and spatially referenced to become a georeferenced raster layer. Once in this format, the geophysical data can be correlated and compared with other forms of georeferenced data (*17*).

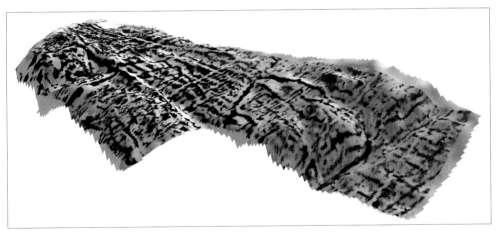

17 Draping geophysical results over a topographic DEM derived from GPS survey – Roman to medieval features at Glendon Hall, Northamptonshire (270 x 180m looking north-west)

GATHERING NEW FIELD DATA

Sometimes, the data that are available from other sources are either inappropriate or limited for a study of a particular landscape and additional data need to be acquired on the ground. In particular, the resolution of available data might be insufficient for a single purpose. This is certainly the case for topographic mapping of sites within their immediate landscapes, or assessing changes to a landscape through repeated surveying over time.

Point, line and polygon data

At the most basic level, the recording of sites may be achieved from sketching positions onto a map to obtain grid references. More sophisticatedly, and depending on the required levels of spatial accuracy, positions of finds or sites might be recorded using a hand-held GPS or triangulated compass position. At the higher resolution end, positions might be recorded using sophisticated survey equipment such as Total Station EDM or Survey Grade Differential GPS (*18*). However the data are collected, the result will normally be a list of coordinates that may be input into the GIS to provide a range of positions that may be analysed directly in terms of distribution, or in relation to other layers of data, such as mapping. Line and polygon data may be generated from these point data within the GIS to provide a graphical representation of features.

The more sophisticated approaches enable elevation to be recorded which can be useful in a number of ways in archaeology, such as considering whether two floors of an excavated building are at the same level, or the interpretation of elevation difference within an industrial complex, to interpret rate of water flow along a channel, for example. Principally, within GIS the point, line and polygon data will form the basis for most types of analysis and can be spatially related to all other types of data obtained from desk-based work.

Topographical data

Whilst elevation might be recorded as part of point, line or polygon data, large quantities of elevation data may be used to generate surfaces within the GIS through different methods of interpolation, in the same way that surfaces may be generated from commercially available topographical data (see above). By surveying a dense scatter of three-dimensional positions across a site or landscape, you provide the potential for creating a much more accurate model of the landscape than would be possible through commercially available data.

Topographical data are collected in the same way as any contour survey would be conducted. Principally, the challenge is to obtain numerous three-dimensional positions across the area of interest. This may be achieved in a grid using an

18 A variety of different equipment may be used for obtaining data for inputting into GIS. This figure shows Trimble's Survey Grade Differential GPS equipment

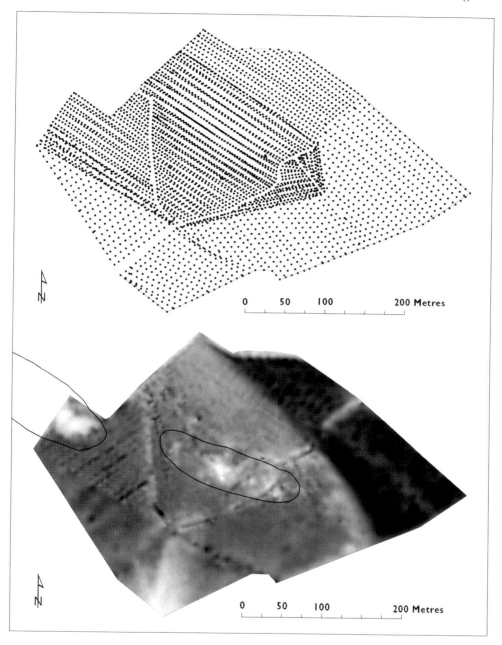

19 Raw data for generating a DEM derived from GPS survey – Meare Village East, Somerset

optical levelling device, or more rapidly through the use of more sophisticated equipment such as Total Station EDM or Differential GPS (*19*).

The ways in which data are collected for creating TINs or raster models in GIS will profoundly influence the usefulness of the resulting model. Before considering the resolution of data collection (i.e. how close together you record positions), it is first necessary to consider whether data will be collected at regular intervals, or following the positions of any earthworks. Clearly, if there are complex earthworks on a site, these are likely to require more recorded positions in order to simulate them in the GIS model than an area of flat land would need. The relative values of 'gridded' and 'non-gridded' data for generating GIS models were considered in a paper by Fletcher and Spicer (1988) who applied contrasting sampling methods to a virtual surface in a simulation study. By recreating the surface from the sampled data the two different approaches were considered (objective and subjective, or gridded and non-gridded). The results from this study demonstrated that, where earthworks are prominent within a landscape, they will need a greater number of points to represent them. If the site is gridded, this provides a very large quantity of points, and thus has implications for survey time. Thus it was concluded that non-gridded survey methods were most appropriate for areas of complex earthworks, whilst other areas could be approached in a more systematic manner. Often it is best to use a combination of systematic and non-systematic survey methods.

Where earthworks are not complex on a site, it is normally most appropriate to collect data in transects across the landscape. The data collection interval should be considerably smaller than the distance over which features visibly change on the ground. Furthermore, it is normally most appropriate to align transects either across the principal alignment of any earthworks (such as ridge and furrow) or at an angle to them, but certainly not straight along them. With modern survey equipment, it is often possible to collect data automatically at a set time or distance interval. A loss of accuracy may be expected using this method due to difficulties in keeping the detail staff level and so forth, although the advantages in terms of time can be extremely positive. Variations in sample resolution along transects might also be different from the distance between transects. This is worth experimenting with, although it is perhaps best to respond to the archaeology on the ground and use the most appropriate method for collecting data that will represent the features on the computer. As a rule of thumb, more data will generate a better model, although the collecting of points very close together does provide the potential for generating a model of local variations that are not reflected on the ground due to the accuracy of the survey equipment and the user. Often this will lead to the need to strip down data to avoid localised artefacts in the resulting GIS model.

ENVIRONMENTAL DATA

So far this chapter has considered archaeological data and cartographic data. In addition to these it is often useful to integrate environmental data into projects. The use of geology and soils maps can be useful in understanding the distributions of archaeological finds and, particularly in the case of aerial photography, understanding the visibility of archaeological features.

As with other maps, geology and soils maps are often available digitally, though not universally, and often not at the range of scales available for other types of maps. Even where they are not available digitally, and copyright permitting, paper copies may be scanned and georeferenced. In this format they may either be used as a raster layer without further processing for comparative purposes, or else the different geological or soils units may be digitised to create a polygon layer. Using the latter approach, either single types of deposit, such as peat, can be digitised, or all features may be digitised to create topologically correct continuous coverages.

Additional environmental data may be obtained from numerous other sources. These might include borehole data, normally inputted into the GIS as a database with different layers incorporated. In the case of numerous boreholes, it can be possible to model different layers as TINs or rasters (*20*).

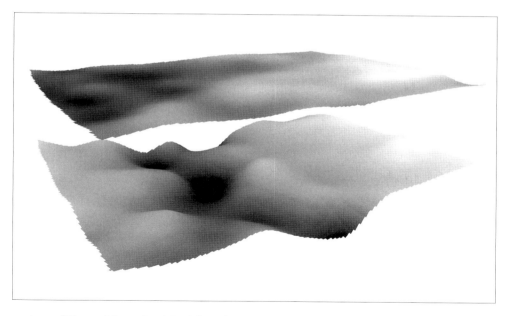

20 Area of Thorne Moors, South Yorkshire, showing the peatland surface and the basal clay topography derived from borehole survey (150 x 190m viewed from the east)

Alternatively environmental data may include bathymetric data. For example, when considering issues such as shifting coastlines or sea-level change, it can be useful to incorporate bathymetric data within the GIS. This may be obtained from sources such as the Admiralty in the UK as paper charts or digitally as sounding points. Whilst issues such as erosion, accretion and dredging will normally have altered the coastline and undersea surface, this still provides a useful starting point for developing models of past landscapes, particularly where a continuous raster model is required. When this is achieved, it becomes possible to model the impact of themes such as sea-level rise through time on the available land area.

CONCLUSIONS

In this chapter, the types of data used in landscape archaeology have been considered in relation to how they might be procured directly for use within a GIS. In addition to the data types outlined in chapter 2, this chapter has also included approaches to collecting new field data, including both survey and palaeoenvironmental data. Both of these themes will be explored further in the following chapters.

5

Processing spatial data

INTRODUCTION

Following on from the previous chapter, the focus of chapter 5 is to finalise the processing stages of GIS, setting it up for further analyses. Chapter 2 identified the types of data that exist for landscape archaeology. Chapter 3 explored themes of spatial data, and chapter 4 brought these themes together by exploring how landscape archaeology datasets may be specifically procured for integration within a GIS environment. In this chapter, the methods of processing spatial datasets within the GIS are explored, including organisation, databases, metadata and the various methods of interpolating from different data sources. The representation of landscape surface models is explored as are the variety of surface analysis tools and how they might usefully be applied within landscape archaeology.

ORGANISING SPATIAL DATA FOR GIS

Different layers of spatial data may be viewed together within the GIS due to the fact that they are linked by the same coordinate system. In order to maintain spatial consistency between different datasets, it is necessary to maintain the same coordinate system for each layer and to ensure that each layer is spatially referenced to the same resolution. In other words, it is possible to provide grid references to a number of different levels of accuracy. With the Ordnance Survey it is necessary to transform the alphabetical prefix to its numerical counterpart. Then, the number of figures for each of the Northings and Eastings will provide levels of accuracy. Hence a 12-figure grid reference (e.g. 459225, 325123) will give accuracies to the metre, such that decimal places will be to the decimetre or centimetre. A shorter grid reference will give lower precision. For example, a 10-figure reference (e.g. 45922, 32512) will provide precision to 10m, with decimal figures providing metre and decimetre values. An 8-figure reference (e.g. 4592, 3251) will provide precision to 100m, with decimals at tens of metres and metres. It is crucial that all datasets are calibrated to the same coordinate system and to the same reference value.

Assuming the spatial referencing of the different datasets to be put into the GIS are consistent, then organising spatial data becomes possible. The ways in which a spatial GIS database may be organised is partially dependent on the software, whereby different layers of data may be associated in particular ways. For example, data may be organised in groups or geodatabases, or particular layers may be referenced so that they will only be shown at particular scales, thus ensuring that layers are used appropriately in relation to their original scale. However, for the purposes of most landscape archaeological approaches, maintaining different layers of data is relatively straightforward, creating maps that contain the layers being used.

A caveat with much GIS study is the way in which data, generated by the GIS from the original input data, may be organised within the GIS. For example, many GIS files will contain a number of different files. In ESRI software, shapefiles relating to point, line or polygon data normally contain five separate files. Similarly, raster files will contain six separate files, with an additional file normally contained elsewhere. For different GIS layers to work correctly, all of these files need to be present, and so the organisation of data within directories on the computer is crucial, particularly if files are to be copied for use on other machines. Similarly, maps that are created will contain information regarding the locations of each of the files being used, in terms of where they are stored on the computer. Thus, copying map files can only be achieved through altering the file itself, or by recreating the map on each separate machine that is used. However, all of these issues will be largely software specific, although it is worth considering these types of issues before designing a GIS database to limit the problems that might be encountered.

DATABASES

GIS is essentially a spatial database that enables new data to be generated from existing data, such as from comparing different layers of data, or through the interrogation of a particular database. The design of GIS databases follows similar principles to all other databases and it is worth some consideration of how databases work so that the best can be made from them. Within GIS software two types of spatial database exist; relational databases and object-oriented databases.

Relational databases are the most common form of data structure, both within and outside of GIS (*21*).

Code	X-coordinate	Y-coordinate	Material	Period	Class	Context
100589	566504	521101	Bronze	MBA	Spearhead	Metal detector
100590	567330	567880	Silver	ROMAN	Coin	Metal detector
100591	581000	543000	–	IA	Hillfort	Aerial photograph
100592	578930	566380	–	PM	Windmill	Document
100593	591100	586630	–	MED	Village	Earthworks
100594	598700	553380	–	?	Crop mark	Aerial photograph
100595	591200	592100	Bronze	LBA	Axe	Antiquarian
100596	585443	521002	–	MED	Church	Standing building
100597	581000	564000	–	?	Enclosure	Aerial photograph
100598	592350	563460	Pottery	ROMAN	Scatter	Fieldwalking

21 A typical archaeological database of sites and finds

A relational database is essentially hierarchical, whereby different elements of the database are related to other sections. To clarify this point, consider the example of a database of locations of pottery found during fieldwalking. The principal spatial database may be a unique identifier, an *x*-coordinate and a *y*-coordinate, thus providing locational information. Once the pottery has been analysed, there might be a separate database consisting of the same unique identifier as the first database, but additional fields for the type of material, the type of artefact and the date from which it was manufactured. In this simple example, it is possible to see that the databases may be joined in relation to the unique identifiers in each table such that, within the GIS, the locational database may be interrogated in relation to the second database. Hence it is possible to provide an illustration of pottery distribution from a particular date or of a particular material. Relational databases are hence based upon relationships, whereby different tables, perhaps constructed as a spreadsheet, a simple table or within database software, are linked or joined together through shared fields, thus creating a much larger database. The advantages of this type of database are that it is a relatively transparent method of organising data and is the most commonly used method. The drawbacks of this type of database are that the data may only be interrogated on the basis of the ways in which it is structured.

The alternative method of database construction is Object-Oriented GIS (OO-GIS). Whilst this remains relatively underused within the archaeological community, it works on the basis of object-oriented programming (see Tschan 1999). Using the traditional data structures of rasters and vectors, archaeological sites need to be significantly simplified to be useful within the GIS. This means that a site will either be represented by a cell with a value of 1, perhaps, within a raster of 0s, or else as a point, line or polygon in a vector format. Thus levels of information about the site are omitted following the required simplification of the site to its abstract form. Sites become reduced to simplified cells or vectors in space, linked to attribute tables providing information about them. In Object-Oriented systems, the approach is to consider the archaeological site or find as closely as it is by an archaeologist, treating each as an object. To take Wheatley and Gillings' (2002) example, one may consider a Bronze Age bell-barrow. From an archaeological perspective, such a monument may be considered to be within a broader class of 'Bronze Age burial mounds' which may be divided into sub-classes of bell-barrow, dish-barrow, saucer-barrow and so forth. In other words, the bell-barrow is a sub-class of Bronze Age burial mounds, which shares similarities with other burial mounds from that period, but differs in terms of shape. Hence, the site is seen within the Object-Oriented database as an object which, in addition to having its own attributes relating to size and so forth, also has non-hierarchical relationships with a range of other monuments and features.

Thus, whilst the use of Object-Oriented GIS within archaeology is in its infancy, it provides the potential for the GIS to simulate archaeology in a much more realistic way, albeit a more complex one.

METADATA

Metadata has already been mentioned in part, although it is worth considering in detail here. So far, a number of potential problems that might occur within a GIS through user error have been noted. An obvious example of this is the use of mapping recorded at a low resolution for calculations at a higher resolution. For example, polygons digitised from 1:50,000 scale mapping might get exported to another user, who might be then using them to make calculations at a much higher scale, without the knowledge that they were originally generated at a lower scale, and thus providing the potential for generating large errors.

In many cases, such as where data have been collected for a single purpose, such limitations of data can normally be appreciated and complied with. However, a potential problem arises when a spatial database is likely to be used for a secondary purpose by a third party. When this happens, knowledge of the limitations and original intentions of the data capture might not follow the dataset and so unknown errors or uncertainties can creep in surreptitiously. One way of avoiding this would be to standardise data formats and scales, although this would be arguably inappropriate for archaeological work. Thus a second method of addressing this has been developed; metadata. Effectively, the role of metadata is to provide a security net for such a situation, to ensure that subsequent users of a dataset are aware of its limitations (Miller and Greenstein 1997, Wise and Miller 1997).

There has been some standardisation of the structure of metadata files. The Dublin Core was developed following three years of international consultation (Gillings and Wise 1998). This model provides 15 principal elements within which to record information. These are: Title, Creator, Subject, Description, Publisher, Contributors, Date (of creation or dissemination), Type (i.e. text, image), Format (i.e. book, CD-ROM, web page), Identifier, Source, Language (i.e. English or French), Relation (i.e. if part of a wider study), Coverage (spatial and temporal), and Rights (copyright information). Recently some GIS software packages have begun to provide an integrated method for recording metadata, whereby files held within the GIS may be tagged with information recorded on pro-forma sheets.

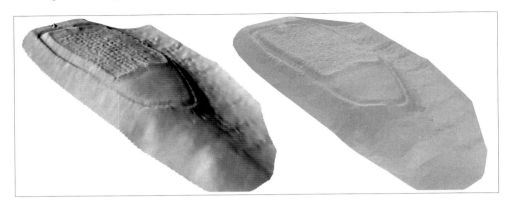

22 Comparing the results of raster interpolation and TIN creation on the Iron Age hillfort site of Conderton Camp, Gloucestershire (280 x 160m viewed from the south-west)

TRIANGULATED IRREGULAR NETWORKS

In chapter 3, the different types of data structure for creating, representing and analysing three-dimensional data were considered, particularly with reference to TINs and rasters. TINs, or more strictly, Triangular Irregular Networks (but also sometimes referred to as Polyhedral Irregular Networks), consider three-dimensional data in a three-dimensional way (*22*).

Essentially, a TIN is a vector-based interpolation which creates a solid surface from input data, either from points (containing some type of elevation attribute) or from contour lines, whereby nodes are used as the key input points. It calculates elevation of a plane passed through the closest data points of known value by joining them with their nearest neighbours by arcs to form polygons. With TINs these polygons are always trianglular. TINs have an advantage insofar as they can generate surfaces from multiple data sources that can include breaklines (which define sudden changes in height). TIN models can be generated directly from either regularly or irregularly spaced input data, so that greater detail may be obtained from one part of a surveyed site than another.

The resulting TIN surface is comprised of triangular facets or planes with the input point data at each of points of the triangle. For irregularly spaced data, the sizes of the triangles will thus vary. The resulting surface is a mesh of triangles held in three-dimensional space dependent on the elevations of the input data. In addition to generating a TIN surface, it is possible to add breaklines into the TIN when it is created. A breakline is any GIS line which represents a direct break in the data. This might relate to a cliff edge, for example. By inputting a breakline into the TIN, the surface will be modelled from each side of the line just up to it, enabling complex landscape features to be modelled accurately.

In addition to the obvious advantages of using breaklines, one of the principal advantages of the TIN data structure is the ability to use a variety of input data together, such as combining point and line data. It is also a useful interpolation method since it only uses the input data and will not generate errors or interpolation artefacts (such as deep pits or peaks) that other methods of interpolation can generate. Similarly, the input data can be of a variety of spatial resolutions, which is extremely useful if you are modelling data resulting from an earthwork survey which contains high-resolution point coverage for areas of earthworks and a lower resolution for the flatter areas. This is because the TIN itself does not assume a particular resolution of its own, in contrast to raster data structures. Once created, the TIN occupies a single file which is extremely useful for simple copying of data files between computers or between different spatial databases.

A TIN may be used for direct surface representation or for surface analyses. For example, TINs can be interrogated directly to obtain information regarding elevation, aspect and slope, or analysed in terms of visibility, determining an observer's view of a landscape from a particular position. However, further than interrogation of the TIN, analyses will generate outputs in the form of rasters, at a given cell resolution (see chapter 3 and below for a discussion of raster formats). For example, a TIN can be used to generate models of slope, aspect, hillshade, viewshed or cut-fill analysis, but the results from these analyses will be rasters.

There are two principal limitations of TIN data structures. Firstly, the surfaces generated from the input data form straight lines and planes between the input points, rather than providing some element of smoothing. This presents a potentially unrealistic representation of a landscape or site, although it can be compensated for through smoothing in some software packages if the TIN is converted or interpolated into a raster data format. The second limitation of TINs is that they lack the mathematical potential for rasters. For example, comparing surfaces mathematically, such as adding surfaces together, or combining surfaces (see below) cannot be achieved within conversion. These mathematical capabilities are among the most powerful tools available within GIS and so often a TIN will ultimately need to be converted to a raster for in-depth analysis.

A TIN's accuracy is dependent upon the process of triangulation that is employed to form a continuous surface. Commonly, an interpolation method known as Delaunay Triangulation will be used which follows a criterion that a circle drawn through the three nodes of each triangle will contain no other data points, thereby requiring smaller triangles in areas of greater point density (*cf.* Voigtmann *et al.* 1997).

Other than the ability to generate surfaces from regularly and irregularly spaced data and from multiple sources (including both contours and points), there are three main benefits to using TINs in the generation of surfaces from point-based data (Goucher 1997, 249-50). Firstly, the Delaunay Triangulation process means that the triangles formed are as equiangular as possible, providing a better geometry than if the angles were able to become more acute. This means that the surfaces are potentially more accurate which is helpful for further analyses. Secondly, the Delaunay process ensures that every interpolated area is as near as possible to a triangle node so a minimum of interpolation is required. Finally, this process gives each survey point equal priority so that the order in which the points are processed will not affect the resulting surface (Goucher 1997: 249). However, although TIN generators have become increasingly popular over the past decade due to their apparent efficiency and flexibility, they are more reliable when the data source consists of irregularly distributed spot heights. When contour data is used they are less reliable, forming a less realistic landscape representation, and can generate errors when modelling valley bottom morphology, requiring subjective breaklines to be added, although some research has been conducted to overcome such errors (e.g. Voigtmann *et al.* 1997). It was also noted that the potential of surface smoothing provided a further paradox insofar as it can reduce artefacts of the interpolation process but will also lose some micro-relief information (Voigtmann *et al.* 1997).

There are two principal ways of converting TINs to raster formats. The first is by direct conversion, whereby a grid of a given surface resolution (or cell size) is effectively draped as a rubber sheet over the TIN, and each cell is given an elevation value taken from the TIN itself. This is the most direct method of generating a raster from a TIN, whilst maintaining the detail that is available within the TIN itself. The second method is through interpolation, whereby the nodal values of the TIN form the basis for generating a mathematically derived surface of cells. The relative merits of the different methods of interpolating surfaces are outlined below.

INTERPOLATION

Of principal importance to GIS cell-based modelling is the DEM and a number of studies have investigated the applications, values and limitations of different raw data sources, ways of creating the DEM, and ways of measuring errors within the DEM (e.g. Burrough 1986, Hutchinson and Gallant 1999). A number of studies have addressed the accuracy of models resulting from the use of different types of data and through different approaches.

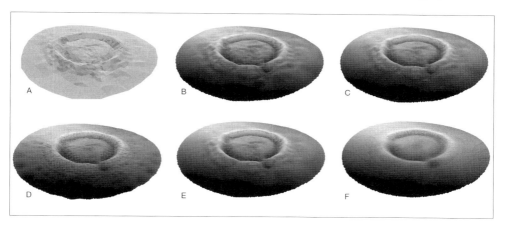

23 The results from different interpolation methods of an earthwork survey: (A) Triangular Irregular Network, (B) Regularised Spline, (C) Tension Spline, (D) Inverse Distance Weighting, (E) Ordinary Kriging, (F) Universal Kriging – Migdale henge, Highlands (area measures 20m across, looking north-west)

Different GIS software packages provide different options for the interpolation of DEMs, although the range may be classified into three main categories – *linear interpolation* (drawing straight lines through data points), *Cubic Spline* (drawing a curve through the data points) and *statistical interpolation* (using algorithms to generate values for cells between known data points based on the values of them) (Gillings and Wise 1998: 35-6). An outline of these various methods is provided in chapter 8 of Burrough (1986). This text describes the mathematical framework of the various techniques, and some of the applications of these methods and their effects. Different interpolation methods will have varying appropriateness for dealing with different types of data and with providing different types of results (*23*).

Trend

Trend describes 'gradual long-range variations' of the *z*-value of a model (Burrough 1986: 149). It uses polynomial regression to generalise the surface from a statistical approach to the raw point data. As such the surface rarely passes through the survey points, but rather provides a model of trend. Defaults normally use a linear trend, although options for non-linear surfaces using quadratic and cubic regression are possible. The effects of these are outlined in Burrough (1986).

This method of surface interpolation is therefore different from the other in that it does not attempt to recreate a landscape, but rather it generalises the data. The usefulness of trend surfaces lies in the possibility of measuring deviation from the general trend. It is therefore not normally considered as an interpolation method (Burrough 1986). Within the present study, trend has been included as a baseline for generalising the dataset and a basis for comparisons with other data.

Spline

Spline interpolation creates a surface from point data by fulfilling two criteria. Firstly, the surface must pass exactly through all data points rather than generalising them. This means that the resulting DEM will retain the more subtle features unlike with the trend function (Burrough 1986). Secondly, the surface must display minimum curvature, creating a continuous and smooth surface (ESRI 1995). An advantage of this technique is that calculations do not require high processing power. Splines can be generated within two principal parameters: either regularised or with tension. The two approaches produce different models, although tension normally will reduce the number of interpolation artefacts from the processes. This method is sometimes referred to as Regularised Spline with Tension (RST).

Inverse distance weighting

Inverse distance weighting (IDW) is a method of interpolating a DEM by calculating the averages of the data around each input-data point. With IDW, this averaging is weighted inversely with distance. For each cell in the DEM, those input-data points closer to the cell are given greater influence on its value than those further away. The effectiveness of this function is dependent upon the size of influence for each cell (Burrough 1986). In other words, changes in the radius used will have a direct effect upon the value of each cell point as more or less data is considered. Greater radii will also increase the need for computing effort. Commonly, the default uses the nearest 12 points to the cell for the calculation, with a maximum radius of five map units.

Kriging

Kriging (or 'optimal interpolation') is an interpolation method that uses spatial covariance to create a statistical surface from point data, based upon factors more complex than the single function of distance demonstrated by spline (Burrough 1986). The technique is most useful when interpolating surfaces from data that is less anomalous for the creation of the DEM. Kriging assumes that regional spatial variation is statistically reflected by the rest of the data and is thus not appropriate for datasets displaying vast local vertical variations, as the surface will be treated as uniform. This is the most advanced interpolation method, relying on a multiple factors rather than just distance.

Generating rasters from TINs

For many purposes, raster data will be required and so a TIN model will need to be converted. Different software packages enable this in different ways. In many GIS packages there is an option to perform a direct conversion from the TIN to the raster. Such a conversion interpolates a continuous grid using the TIN as a reference from which gridded elevations are calculated. The function places a grid of cells at a pre-determined density across the area covered by the TIN which are referenced in terms of x and y coordinates. A height attribute for each cell is then interpolated from the TIN. ArcInfo presents a number of different ways of converting a TIN to a lattice using this function, the primary two being linear and quintic interpolation. Linear interpolation treats the TIN's arcs between nodes as straight lines that are reflected directly in the heights of the cells across it. The areas enclosed by the TIN's triangles are then treated as flat plates. Surfaces constructed using linear interpolation often look faceted and unnatural, though the potential for interpolation inaccuracies is reduced. The second main method, quintic interpolation, applies smoothing to the areas inside of the TIN triangles. This method appreciates that the surface being represented is smooth without the harsh breaks in slope represented through linear interpolation. Instead a continuous smooth surface is created which runs through the nodes and forms a smooth interpolation through the areas between. The resultant surface is not only more aesthetically realistic, but has the potential for being more accurate with a curved, rather than faceted, surface. Similar processes are provided in ArcInfo using Tinlattice, in ArcGIS using the 'convert' function, or in IDRISI using Tinsurf.

DEM RESOLUTION

The relationship between the data source and the DEM extends further than the choice of interpolation/generation method to be used. DEM resolution is crucially important and may be defined as the size of each cell in x and y (24).

Principally, the DEM resolution directly influences the degree to which it is suitable for a specific application (Veregin 1999). The value of each method of interpolation is dependent on the input-data source and the desired cell size of the resulting grid. It has been shown, however, that general trends exist. For example, a paradox exists within grid interpolation techniques such that computer processing power and data storage can be a problem if a large area is analysed at high resolution (i.e. small cell size). If a lower resolution is chosen then the DEM can become inaccurate and over-generalised (Carrara *et al.* 1997), and may negatively affect analyses (Madry and Rakos 1996).

24 The results from interpolating a DEM at the different surface resolutions of 10m, 5m and 0.5m – Breamore, Hampshire (260 x 150m area looking south-west)

Studies have also highlighted the effect of the relative resolution of the data source (*cf.* João 1998) and the desired cell size within cell-based DEMs. Gao (1997) chose three landscapes displaying the different topographic characteristics of a valley, a peak and a ridge, and generated DEMs from digitised contours interpolated into a grid through kriging. The accuracy of each resulting DEM was analysed in relation to the real landscape that was being represented by the model. The tests also investigated the impact of interpolating at different cell resolutions. In order to standardise the results of the experiments, each DEM was analysed to explore the effects of the variable contour resolution and DEM cell size through examining gradient in different areas of the models. The results of this research demonstrated the minimal effects of resolution on gradient and provided a method for achieving optimal surface resolution from a given contour density.

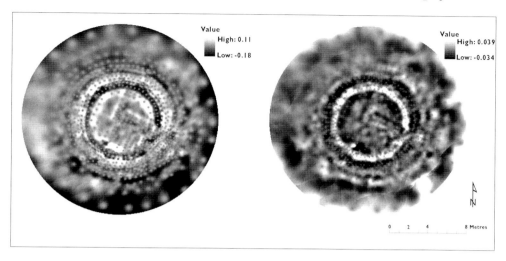

25 Differences between different interpolation techniques. From a dataset with an elevation variation of 1.01m, the difference between Tension Spline and Ordinary Kriging is 0.07m (on the left), whereas the difference between Regular Spline and IDW is 0.29m (on the right)

MEASURING ERROR

A distinguishing feature of GIS is its ability to create new data from input data, achieved by applying algorithms to the data. For example, a DEM may be created from raw variable resolution input data, and the resulting DEM will form the basis for further computations and analyses. Therefore, the accuracy of results from all later levels of analysis is dependent upon the accuracy of the creation of the DEM in the first instance. The possibilities of error may become compounded as further levels of analysis are conducted (25).

It is for this reason that the accuracy of the original data, the *intrinsic* data, is as high as possible. It is also important to scrutinise the validity of the algorithms and processes that are used to generate the new data. This may be referred to as *operational* error (see Marozas and Zack 1990 for error definitions, *cf.* Heuvelink 1999). Finally, it is important to be able to assess whether any errors have been encountered, particularly within the operational process, since these can be corrected. While the abstraction of the landscape into GIS models is advantageous, allowing analyses to be performed on the model which would be impossible on the ground, this same principle means that models cannot be accurately compared to real landscapes in order to check for error. Therefore other methods have been proposed by different researchers to establish ways of checking the accuracy of DEMs and the analytical processes, and thereby their reliability within further analyses. For example, a method using progressive thinning of the input data was applied to assess changes in the DEM in relation to both surface area (compared to its simple two-dimensional planimetric area) and volume (Brasington *et al.* 2000).

It is important to understand where errors occur within a DEM due to the surface's fundamental influence on the results of further analyses (Kvamme 1990). Fisher (1999) highlighted the range of errors that may occur within GIS, classifying *error, vagueness* and *ambiguity*, relating error with *uncertainty*. This work demonstrated the need for users to be aware of these issues in order to provide confidence in their decision-making.

The main problems of such analyses lie in the lack of benchmarks by which to compare abstract data models. The first obstacle is that a model can only be as good as the raw data from which it is derived, and therefore its accuracy can only effectively be compared with this original dataset. Such a comparison has been attempted statistically (e.g. Li 1994) and visually (e.g. Wood and Fisher 1993). The overall quality of the resulting DEM has been examined in a number of ways. Gao (1997), for example, measured the accuracy of 200 randomly chosen points from a given terrain to enter into a statistical equation to calculate root-mean-square-error. Haigh (1993) analysed his resulting DEMs in relation to reliability, robustness and realism. Reliability was measured through the application of the technique to a number of different sites. Robustness was seen in relation to the required job of the model, in this case the rectification of aerial photographs, and realism was measured by a comparison between the model and the perceived surface it represented. He also noted that large changes could be identified when surfaces were interpolated from contours depending upon the number of points used to digitise them, and through the addition of extra data points. Amongst other methods, Carrara *et al.* (1997) analysed a DEM by comparing the contours that formed the source data for the model and the contours generated from it. In this study five parameters were identified for assessing accuracy. Firstly, cells near to contours should be of similar height; secondly, between contours all cells should be within the vertical range displayed by them; thirdly, in these areas heights should vary linearly between elevations; fourthly, in areas of low relief variability the cell values should reflect a '*realistic* morphology'; and lastly, the distribution of interpolation artefacts should be small (*Ibid.*: 453). Similarly, a further dimension to assessing DEM accuracy was provided by López (1997) who demonstrated that two types of errors were present within DEMs: systematic, resulting from the method used to generate the DEM, and random, resulting mostly from the user (*cf.* Beard and Buttenfield 1999). This research presented a new methodology for identifying random errors by using Principal Component Analysis that was tested by analysing user-generated random errors. A statistical approach to measuring the probability of error across a DEM has been suggested

(Kyriadis *et al.* 1999). This method produced alternative representations of other possible outcomes for areas not covered by what was referred to as 'hard' data, or input data.

SURFACE REPRESENTATION

The representation of digital surfaces can provide information regarding the nature of the landscape and has the potential to provide information about micro-topography that may reflect archaeological and non-archaeological activity. Surfaces can be represented in two ways, centred on whether or not elevation is displayed.

Elevation-based surfaces

Elevation-based surfaces display models such that their vertical scale is represented (*colour plate 3*). Typical methods of display include contours and contour bands whereby ranges in vertical drop are generalised by a given symbol. The advantage of such methods is that they display features that highlight vertical drops such as river valleys and assist in the understanding of the landscape.

On a basic level, elevation surfaces may be represented as contour lines or bands. Contour lines are usually positioned at given intervals in order to provide a linear representation of height. Contour bands can fulfil the same job, but can also be scaled mathematically from the data. Archaeological features are normally identified as being anomalous compared with the surrounding landscape. Linear contour bands generalise a landscape and therefore limit the visibility of surface detail. Within landscapes where archaeology lies upon a relatively flat plane, it is possible that features will lie within a single contour band and as such will not be visible. In these cases, a second method of contour banding may be applied based upon percentiles of the frequency of different cell values.

Non-elevation-based surfaces

Non-elevation surface representations display detail of topographic change, highlighting subtleties of the surface itself rather than in changes in elevation. It has the added advantage of representing details that may be missed, lying between contour values, for example. There are several methods of non-elevation-based surface representation. The first illuminates the surface from a given lighting position (an analytical function, though considered here under the heading of representation, but which could equally be considered within surface analysis). Hillshading is a method of improving the visual quality of a map (*colour plate 4*). It calculates areas of light and shade by determining reflectance of the source based upon elements of aspect and slope (see below, Burrough 1986). The result of such analysis is a surface that is similar aesthetically to aerial photographs, highlighting earthworks, for example. By altering the position of the light source it is possible to highlight alternative features.

The second main method included within the theme of non-elevation surface representation is perspective modelling, using elements such as elevation exaggeration and draping of vector and raster features on a wire-frame mesh. Principally, this is achieved through identifying a DEM as the surface, multiplying the values of each cell by a given exaggeration value, and draping a mesh (or other data) over it. This is represented from a given angle, with an observer position and a target position, providing an oblique perspective image. The advantage of this representation method is that the less pronounced features will be highlighted with the altered ratio between the Cartesian coordinates and the height values. Further, the perspective model provides a backdrop for draping other archaeological features, providing a clearer visual understanding of the relationship between topography and archaeology.

SURFACE ANALYSIS TOOLS

A DEM surface can be analysed in a number of ways before any layers of data are added to it, but also in relation to other layers of data (such as archaeological distributions). Surfaces can be generalised by calculating slope or aspect, or more complex analyses of visibility can be used. Surface analyses such as slope and aspect can form a basis for understanding the surface, particularly in relation to DEMs based on survey data of archaeological earthwork sites. The latter, more complex types of analysis using visibility are often used for the interpretation of archaeological landscapes, but have also been used in relation to assessing the impact of development. Approaches involving surface analyses are common, particularly within studies using multiple techniques to understand terrain form in relation to archaeological distribution (e.g. Kvamme 1992).

Slope
Slope has been defined as the combination of both gradient (the maximum rate of change in altitude) and aspect (compass direction of gradient) (*cf.* Burrough 1986: 50). The calculation of slope creates a new raster with values relating to the gradient for each cell (*colour plate* 5). The output grid is defined either in terms of percentage or degree and is calculated from the greatest change in height between the cell in question and the eight cells immediately surrounding it. Slope, along with elements of elevation, has been used to investigate location

preference in past occupation distributions (e.g. Kuna and Adelsbergerová 1995), providing both CRM and interpretative results. Calculations of slope have been a principle aspect of multiple surface analyses, particularly those involving predictive modelling (e.g. Kohler and Parker 1986, Carmichael 1990, Marozas and Zack 1990, Kuna and Adelsbergerová 1995) and interpretative cost-surface analyses (*cf.* van Leusen 1999, Bell and Lock 2000, De Silva and Pizziolo 2001).

Aspect

The calculation of aspect within a DEM identifies the direction of the maximum rate of change in values of each cell (*colour plate 6*). Ascribed cell values are given in positive degrees from north. Archaeologically, it may be argued that elements such as south-facing slopes within the northern hemisphere may be preferentially settled or farmed due to increased solar exposure. Therefore an exploration of correlation between aspect and site distribution may present interesting results in relation to this hypothesis. An example of the use of aspect modelling was provided by Llobera (1996) who generated an aspect model of the Wessex chalklands and compared it to the distribution of linear ditches. This, coupled with other analyses identifying hillcrests, was used to explore the relationship between anthropogenic and natural boundaries. It was noted that there was a positive correlation between changes in aspect and turn in the ditches.

As with slope analysis, the generation of aspect models has been used as one of several layers of data within multiple surface analyses of CRM predictive modelling (e.g. Altschul 1990, Kvamme 1992).

Visibility

Visual analysis on a DEM can be conducted in two ways. Lines of sight (LOS) can be calculated in the binary sense, investigating whether two points are inter-visible, or complete directional or non-directional viewsheds can be calculated from a given position (*26*). The former measures whether obstructions lie between two given points, and the latter calculate all cells that have a clear line of sight from the observation point. The GIS calculates a viewshed for a given position from which rays are sent out to all cells of the DEM. The output of the process is a binary map showing which cells are obstructed, and which are visible.

GIS viewshed analysis has been criticised in a number of ways, including assessments of the nature of accuracy at an algorithmic level (e.g. De Floriani and Magillo 1999). Otherwise, the main focus of criticism has been with the unrealistic binary output that does not reflect the complexities of reality (e.g. Fisher 1992, 1993). In response to this problem, other methods have been applied in order to provide a more realistic understanding of visibility, particularly

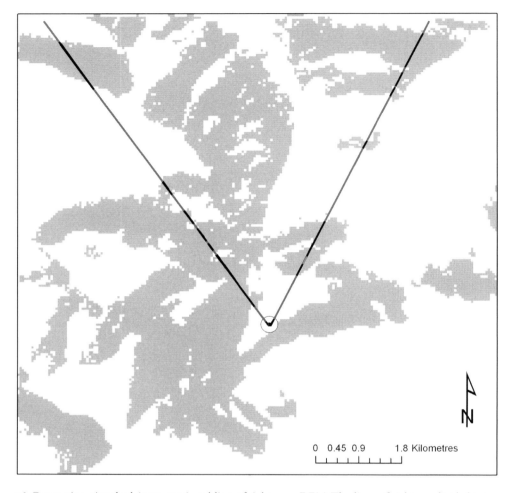

26 Comparing viewshed (grey areas) and line of sight on a DEM. The lines of sight are divided into grey (invisible) and black (visible) areas

in relation to visual impact assessments for new developments. For example, Nackaerts *et al.* (1999) demonstrated an approach that combined a surface representing error within the parent DEM to provide a more realistic calculation of the likely visibility from each cell using probability.

The application of visibility analysis within landscape archaeology is well founded (e.g. Devereux 1991, Thomas 1993, Tilley 1994). The principles upon which visual analyses of this type rest are those of existence and perception. Contemporary studies in the social sciences have suggested that visibility is the principal way in which humans relate to and interpret their landscapes (e.g. Punter 1982). Equally, it has been argued that such interpretations are only possible with a prior understanding of the landscape so that the signs may be interpreted (*cf.* Meinig 1979, Tuan 1979, Cosgrove 1989). Archaeologically, visibility has been an element that may be investigated and understood (e.g. Bender *et al.* 1997) and has been used frequently within interpretative approaches.

For the purposes of most studies a height of 1.7m is chosen for the height of the observer when performing visual analyses. Whilst this is the normal default height used for visibility analyses, it may be corroborated through the analysis of skeletal remains. For example, on the Yorkshire Wolds a number of prehistoric cemeteries have been excavated providing a large population sample, particularly for the early Iron Age (e.g. Stead 1991). A statistical analysis of these skeletal remains was presented by Leese (1991) who has compared the results from this region to broadly contemporary sites elsewhere in the country. The results demonstrated that, in the Yorkshire region, mean heights of individuals represented in the cemeteries were 1.71m for males and 1.58m for females, based upon excavated cemetery populations of 68 and 48 individuals respectively. This figure is slightly high compared to the other sites of Wetwang on the Wolds which produced figures of 1.67m and 1.56m from populations of 122 and 168 individuals, and Maiden Castle which produced figures of 1.65m and 1.52m from populations of 19 and 9 individuals. The figure of 1.7m has been rounded up from the data for males. Clearly other influencing factors including clothing and vegetation will influence the accuracy of level of sight, and so a more accurate determination may not be appropriate.

Combining surface analyses

The results from different surface analyses in isolation can provide valuable information regarding questions relating to landscape archaeology. However, most often the most significant results stem from a process of combined analyses, integrating what each of the different surface analyses techniques show together (*27*).

There are a number of ways of achieving such a comparison of results within the GIS whilst maintaining the original rasters. One method is to examine the different resulting models within a three-dimensional viewer, although a more straightforward method is to explore transparency functions within the software. In most GIS packages it is possible to add a level of transparency to one or more layers of data. This allows numerous surfaces to be viewed simultaneously. For example, for many purposes it will be important to view elevation data in conjunction with surface analysis data such as slope or hillshade. By making the latter models semi-transparent they may be viewed over the top of the elevation surface. Thus, additional details can be identified through the combination which might not have been visible otherwise. This type of approach is particularly useful for examining high-resolution surface data derived from survey or LIDAR.

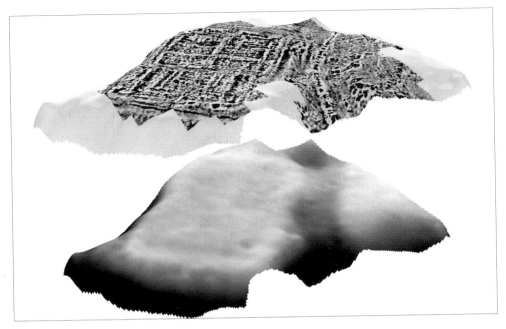

27 Combining topographic modelling (from GPS survey) with the results from geophysical survey at Drumlanrig Roman fort in Dumfries and Galloway (250 x 220m viewed from the east. The area of the fort measures approximately 190 x 120m)

CONCLUSIONS

In this chapter issues of data have been considered. These have included the nature of archaeological data and how this may be integrated usefully within a GIS. Methods of dealing with GIS data, and particularly the use of landscape topographical data, have been considered. Different types of input data have been outlined, and the ways in which these may be processed in order to generate surfaces from them has been covered, including both vector-based surfaces as TINs and raster, cell-based surfaces. This chapter has also considered the relative merits of different ways of representing surface data, and the different ways of analysing it, to generate landscape models of slope, aspect or visibility.

In this and the preceding chapters, the ways in which GIS works with different types of data have been addressed, including how they may be processed and analysed, the issues involved in terms of error, and the various methods of generating new data. This provides a foundation for addressing direct issues of landscape archaeology. This is the first section of the book, addressing method and procedure. The following section of the book addresses these themes, considering questions and case studies relating directly to landscape archaeology.

In the following chapters, the types of analysis already discussed will be considered directly in relation to themes within landscape archaeology. In the next chapter, methods of analysing landscape archaeology are considered from both two-dimensional and three-dimensional approaches. This is followed in chapter 7 by a consideration of landscape reconstruction, including themes of palaeo-vegetation as well as archaeological reconstruction. Chapter 8 then considers themes of theoretical approaches to landscape archaeology, assessing the ways in which GIS users have addressed themes of archaeological theory, and presenting case studies of how theoretical concepts may be addressed using GIS. Chapter 9 brings together many of the separate themes from chapters 6-8, but addressing the interpretation of archaeological landscapes more holistically. Chapter 10 then considers these themes in relation to cultural resource management (CRM), and the ways in which GIS is, and can be, used for addressing the needs of curators. In chapter 11 some new methods for presenting the results of GIS analyses are discussed in relation to the variety of end users of GIS technology.

6

Landscape analysis

INTRODUCTION

In chapter 1, landscape archaeology was defined as being an amalgamation of three principal branches. The first of these was 'landscape analysis', essentially based in the realm of analysing the data that exists for a landscape, commonly performed through activities such as map regression. In other words, the landscape archaeologist in this field will typically be looking for themes and patterns within the landscape, such as field morphology, to assess how the landscape has developed through time and which elements may be attributed to a particular period.

In the previous chapters, themes including space, procuring data, processing data, and ways in which space is considered within a GIS have been examined. This chapter begins to consider how GIS may be used in practical scenarios drawing on a number of case studies and examples. Traditionally the broad theme of landscape archaeology, which may be termed 'landscape analysis', has represented those areas of archaeology that have been concerned with maps and the recognition of the morphology of archaeological features. Whilst this area of landscape archaeology will be considered, additional themes will be drawn upon that lie within what may be termed a positive archaeology, including predictive mapping of archaeological features based on observed data.

TRADITIONAL APPROACHES TO LANDSCAPE ANALYSIS

Landscape analysis is a broad term encompassing a range of activities. For the purposes of this book, landscape analysis is taken to include those areas of archaeology that focus on the interpretation of features in the landscape including identification, mapping and the consideration of principal themes. These include assessing the density of sites and their distribution, considering this distribution in relation to other archaeological or natural features, or analysing archaeological site positions in relation to the archaeological and topographical landscape.

Traditionally such landscape analysis has centred on map work, normally in two-dimensions. Input data have consisted largely of aerial photographs, modern and historical maps, and archaeological data gathered on the ground or obtained from record offices. Approaches to analysing this data have normally consisted of identifying and mapping features, such as crop marks, considering phasing in the landscape between different editions of mapping, and through examining where sites are in relation to natural features. The outputs from much of this type of landscape analysis have been in the form of distribution plots of sites in an area and textual descriptions of trends and findings. Where it has been approached, further analysis might have involved considering the territorial boundaries based upon distributions or examining spheres of influence, although the types of approach are linked closely with trends within archaeological theory.

MAPS, REGRESSION AND GIS

One of the principal tenets of any landscape study is the use of maps. As mentioned in chapter 4, cartographic data includes modern mapping, historical mapping and environmental mapping, such as geology or soils maps. Maps are clearly a good point of departure for any study using a cartographic software package such as GIS. As mentioned in chapter 1, one method of approaching landscapes is to regress them. In other words, the approach is to identify datable features within an area, such as a Roman road, and remove them gradually to reveal the earlier landscapes beneath them. Commonly this is approached by analysing the stratigraphic relationships between features, such as a motorway, interrupting the field pattern.

Within GIS, this type of approach may be addressed by generating themed or dated layers based on vector formats. How this is achieved depends largely on the nature of the input data. For vector-based maps, it is normally possible to select features of a given data and to export them to a new file relating to a given period. For raster-based map formats, it will be necessary to digitise the field boundaries and other features of interest. Commonly, a regression analysis aimed at identifying different phases of landscape development will be based upon multiple maps, including both modern and historical maps. In these cases a combination of vector and raster formats will be required, necessitating an approach using georeferencing, digitising of features and vector selection.

IDENTIFICATION OF FEATURES

A second branch of landscape analysis involves the identification and interpretation of morphologically distinct features. This process can also involve the identification of different phases of activity on a site and is commonly undertaken through survey work. For example, the work of the Royal Commission on the Historical Monuments have perfected the process of hachured survey (e.g. Bowden 1999) aimed at identifying features, phasing etc. The advantages of this approach lie in the interpretative approach that involves a high level of archaeological skill.

> Hachure plans are a useful and well understood notation within archaeology and can be used to create a clear visual representation of terrain form that would be difficult to represent using contours (Wheatley and Gillings 2002, 108).

However, limitations exist with this traditional method of notation. Firstly, they are a purely qualitative approach, representing only relative variation in terrain rather than absolute height. Secondly, they tend to focus on interpreted detail at the expense of broader topographical trends. Thirdly, hachure plans can become so densely drawn and complex that the results are rendered effectively meaningless (Wheatley and Gillings 2002). Consequently, in the context of GIS, hachured plans are limited to their use as a georeferenced image. 'Hachure plans are best regarded as a form of interpretation or presentation rather than as a formal method of recording' (Wheatley and Gillings 2002, 110).

In contrast to the hachured survey is a contour survey. If the hachured survey is subjective, then the contour survey may be considered objective, although the realities of this are more variable. The idea is to record three-dimensional positions across a site in order to reconstruct a contour representation. Within a GIS, and through various surface interpolation techniques, it is possible to generate a 'solid' surface model rather than, or in addition to, contours (*28*). With the development of survey equipment, and particularly GPS, the capturing of data has become extremely rapid enabling high resolutions to be achieved. In chapter 4, the advantages and problems involved with data capture using such methods were outlined, highlighting the need to respond to the local topography, choosing the appropriateness of systematic or irregular recording of positions. In addition, different interpolation methods will produce different results from different types of data.

Commercially available data, from either the Ordnance Survey, or from remotely-sensed data, is often at a resolution that is too low for the representation of archaeological features and particularly earthworks. Thus through accurate survey aimed at obtaining three-dimensional positions across the area of study,

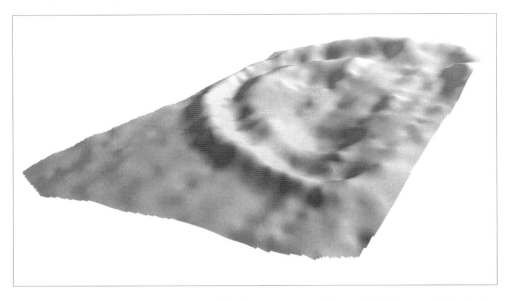

28 Cockhill, Blackpatch, West Sussex. Model of a Bronze Age enclosure identifying morphologically diagnostic features

it is possible to generate Digital Elevation Models (DEMs) of these features. This might be undertaken for a number of reasons. At the most basic level, the approach might be to record features three-dimensionally, with the added advantage of generating a plan that may facilitate interpretation (*cf.* Bowden 1999). If the morphology of a site has been compromised, perhaps through erosion, ploughing or environmental changes (e.g. peat growth, alluviation or even vegetation growth), the features are commonly less visible on the ground, and so a second theme of identifying the more subtle features might be appropriate. Thirdly, additional detail may be required for interpretation purposes. It might be important to identify subtle features through surface analysis that might assist in the interpretation of a site. Many archaeological sites will have various needs in terms of interpretation. While spatial areas may require a combination of approaches, here those approaches will be addressed separately.

Recording morphology

A high-resolution survey of an area of upstanding earthworks will provide data for modelling a surface within the GIS, in addition to generating a point-in-time record of the site. However, this will be dependent upon the usefulness of collected points. As mentioned previously, a study of 'Clonehenge' identified the need for examining the usefulness of regularly spaced and non-regularly space survey data (Fletcher and Spicer 1988). This study demonstrated that, within an

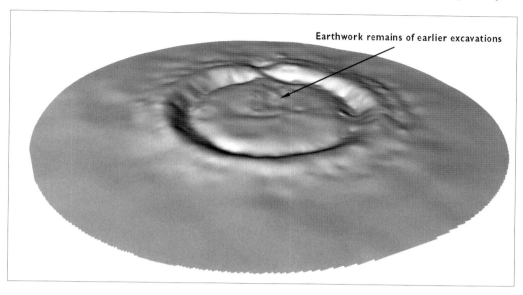

Earthwork remains of earlier excavations

29 Hillshaded DEM of the hengiform monument at Loch Migdale, Highlands, showing the position of an earlier excavation trench (20 x 20m looking east-south-east)

area of archaeological earthworks, local variations in topography can be high over a small area. The recording of regular survey positions for generating a DEM would therefore require an exceptionally high resolution, and thus a high number of points. Consequently, it was argued that a varied approach should be used, responding to the local needs of the archaeology to ensure that breaks in slope are fully represented. For the purposes of recording morphology of the earthworks of a site, this may be taken as a useful rule of thumb.

The aims of recording morphology may be reduced to two basic elements. There is the need to generate a record of the site that may have archival value and which can assist in the interpretation of a site through seeing it in plan, as some archaeological sites are very difficult to fully comprehend and interpret on the ground. An example of this is the hengiform monument from the northern edge of Loch Migdale, near Tain, in the Scottish Highlands (*29*).

Here, a small prehistoric monument was already known and was visible on the ground, and had been partially excavated previously. A rapid differential GPS survey of the site generated a plot of positions from the surface in advance of excavation that would lose this surface information. nine hundred and sixty-two points were recorded across the site, at a variable surface resolution of between 0.2-2m, becoming more widely spaced in the area outside the monument. The total area of the site measured approximately 20m in diameter, providing an average survey point density of 3.2 points per square metre. The data were processed within the GIS using a spline interpolation technique to generate a DEM relative to absolute heights. The resulting DEM forms a useful record of the site prior to losing surface information from excavation. It also provided a position for the site (which deviated considerably from the Ordnance Survey position in this remote area) and a plan, although in this case some interpretation of the site was possible due to the earthworks being highly visible on the ground. In addition, however, the resulting DEM highlighted the positions of the previous archaeological trenches across the interior of the feature as subtle depressions that were not recognised on the ground.

Identifying subtle features

Sometimes archaeological features may be masked by vegetation or simply by the density of later archaeological features around them. In these cases it is possible to use the high-resolution survey of three-dimensional positions, mentioned previously in relation to the recording of features, with the addition of surface analyses and exaggeration to identify features of interest. For example, Bronze Age features in the Peak District near Carsington reservoir cover large swathes of the landscape, but are masked by the activities of post-medieval miners who excavated numerous bell pits to extract lead (*30*).

One example demonstrated a close relationship between an earlier Bronze Age barrow and a middle-late Bronze Age field boundary. These subtle features were overwhelmed by a mine that had generated dramatic earthworks which dominated the landscape rendering the Bronze Age features less visible on the ground, and even harder to translate to others in any visual way. Effectively, you can't see the wood for the trees, or rather the Bronze Age features for the bell pits! Again, a GPS survey of the site and surrounding area was undertaken at a varying surface resolution to respond to the local variations in topography generated by the different earthwork features. The resulting DEM of the site provided a more convenient illustration of the site, but remained plagued by the same problems of interpretation as on the ground. However, a series of surface analyses made the Bronze Age features more visible. Contouring the model provided the shape of the barrow, distinct from the later features. This showed the shape of the barrow and the difference in morphology compared with the other monuments. The addition of a light source, positioned perpendicular to the alignment of the Bronze Age field boundary served to highlight this feature, despite its being cut through by the later bell pits. The resulting model again provided an accurate record of the site prior to its excavation and also served as an illustration of the different period features and their complex archaeological stratigraphy.

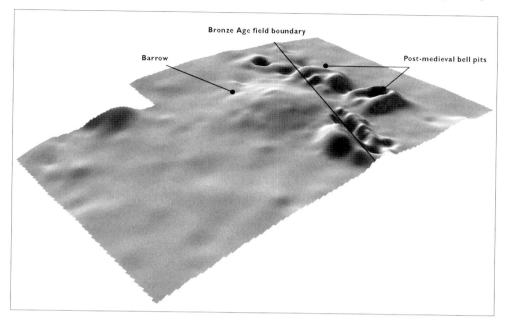

30 Features from a variety of periods represented in a DEM of an area of Carsington pastures, Derbyshire (90 x 65m viewed from the south-east)

Highlighting additional detail

In some cases, a site cannot be fully understood on the ground. Tree coverage, sheer scale and physical damage to a site, such as from ploughing, will render archaeological features invisible on the ground. However, as before, high-resolution surface survey may be used to generate a DEM in the GIS which can then be manipulated in order to obtain maximum information from it. Two examples will be considered here. The first is a medieval motte and bailey site at Beaudesert, in Henley in Arden, Warwickshire, where construction commenced in the twelfth century (*31*).

This site has previously been considered to be unusual archaeologically due to the presence of two baileys rather than the standard one. This interpretation had been based upon previous surveys of the site (Salter 1992). A topographic survey, using a combination of GPS and EDM total station equipment to cope with dense tree coverage in some parts of the site, was undertaken providing 4508 points over an area of 4.43ha. These points were then modelled to generate a DEM within the GIS. Due to the position of the site on the top of a steep hill, all elevation-based rendering of the DEM proved to be of little value. The spread of colour contours for different elevations generalised much of the archaeology, although this was assisted through light shading. However, the best results for the interpretation of

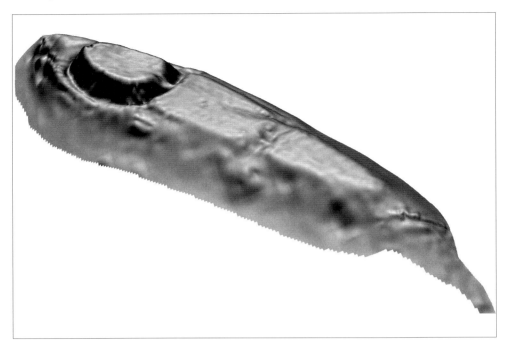

31 Slope model of Beaudesert Castle, Warwickshire, with darker shades representing steeper slopes (450 x 130m looking east)

this model came from slope analyses. Using standard slope-based surface analysis of the DEM, a model displaying steepness by colour shades was generated. This had the advantage of highlighting sudden changes in topography that are common with anthropogenic earthwork features, without the directionality assumed through light-based modelling and shading. From this analysis a number of conclusions were made. Firstly, the slope model highlighted the difference between the steep hillslopes and the flatter hilltop, which would have been occupied by the castle features. Secondly, it showed the positions of archaeological features. These included the ditches across the site and a track running around its western side. Thirdly, the slope model revealed details about the structure of the ditches surrounding the motte area (although it should be noted that the motte in this instance was a separated area of land, rather than being a mound). Part way down the ditches, a line on the slope model indicated a change in slope between the upper section and the lower section. Upon closer examination, this was interpreted as a second phase of ditch digging, with the earlier ditch being shallower and U-shaped and the later ditch being more steeply cut into the base of the earlier one. The later ditch was also steeper in profile. Finally, and perhaps most significantly, the outer bailey was demonstrated to be a natural feature. It was not a second bailey as it had at first

32 Sutton Common, South Yorkshire, from the ground. The remains of the enclosures are extremely difficult to identify

appeared to be due to its flat plateau (a function of geology) and the position of a pathway running around its western side. There were no earthworks forming its eastern side. This was later verified and corroborated through excavation.

A second example is the wetland Iron Age site of Sutton Common, South Yorkshire, where bulldozing and ploughing have removed the majority of the upstanding earthworks such that much of the site is not visible on the ground (*32*).

The site consists of a pair of enclosures occupying islands on opposite sides of a palaeochannel (Whiting 1936, Parker Pearson and Sydes 1997). Of the two enclosures, the smaller is largely intact, surviving as earthworks, whereas the larger enclosure has been completely removed by the bulldozing and ploughing such that it cannot be seen on the ground. A GPS survey of the site provided the data for GIS modelling of the surface. The basic elevation-based surface highlighted the shape of the ploughed-out enclosure. However, through the application of hillshading from the north-west, subtle features were identified, particularly along the western edge of the larger enclosure (*33*). Slight changes in gradient had occurred through the shrinkage of organic sediment within the ditch causing a fall in the height of the overlying land surface. This subtle difference was identified as a linear ditch by hillshading of the DEM (Chapman and Van de Noort 2001).

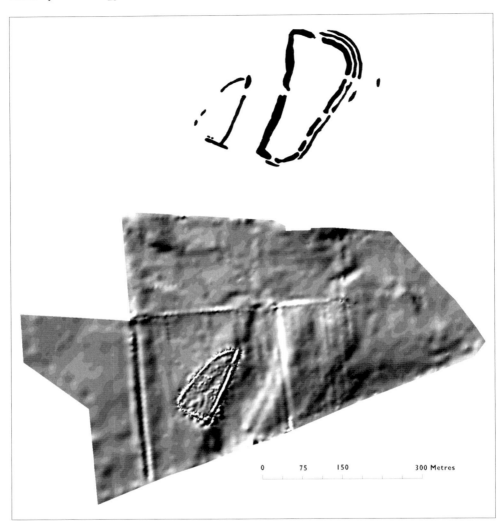

33 Hillshaded DEM of Sutton Common, South Yorkshire, showing the upstanding earthworks of the smaller enclosure and the ploughed-out features of the larger enclosure. Whilst the features of the larger enclosure were not visible on the ground, they could be identified from the GIS model derived from high-resolution GPS survey

LOCAL LANDSCAPE CONTEXT OF FEATURES

As explored in chapter 1, the definition of 'landscape' within the discipline of landscape archaeology is diverse, particularly in terms of spatial scale. A site may be examined in isolation, within its locale (which itself will be variable) or within its wider region, including other sites. When considering the local landscape context of a site, one may refer to the direct physical or anthropogenic features that define it. For example, this might be a slope into which a house platform is cut which will provide the necessary context in order to understand the morphology of the platform itself. In the previous section, reference was made to the wetland Iron Age site of Sutton Common. This provides a good example of a site within its local landscape context, modelled from GPS data. Here the archaeology is defined by earthworks, both upstanding and levelled. Within the wetland landscape, the archaeology only really makes sense in relation to the local topography and palaeo-landscape features. The two enclosures occupy areas of higher land, effectively islands above the surrounding marshy wetlands. Running between the two 'islands' is a relict palaeochannel, which again would have been much wetter during the Iron Age and the period of occupation. The survey of the site covered the local landscape surrounding the enclosures. In addition to identifying the subtleties of the earthworks (see above), the GIS modelling of the site also demonstrated how the morphology of the earthworks reflected the natural morphology of the 'islands', and also highlighted the surrounding wetland landscape, including the palaeochannel, other islands and a deep wetland area to the east of the archaeology (Chapman and Van de Noort 2001) (*colour plate 7*). A plan of the site without this three-dimensional element of the landscape could not convey the detail of the site, which equally remains hard to understand on the ground. Such an understanding is crucial before the analysis of the landscape archaeology of the site becomes possible.

THE WIDER LANDSCAPE CONTEXT OF FEATURES

Moving outwards from the local context of features, the wider context may include almost any resolution of study that seems appropriate for a given question. This might range from local to national concerns, though normally, particularly when dealing with three-dimensional landscape modelling, the wider landscape context of features may for the present purposes be defined as an area of between 5 x 5km and 30 x 30km. This convenient, though arbitrary, division between the local landscape and the wider landscape may more appropriately be defined by the nature of the landscape archaeology, or perhaps the input data being used for the study. Typically, though not always, the input data for local landscape studies will be generated by ground survey, whereas data for the wider landscape is more likely to be purchased commercially, such as from national mapping agencies (e.g. the Ordnance Survey) or from remotely-sensed data (e.g. LIDAR). From these types of data it becomes possible to explore the relationships between different sites rather than the context of a single site, though not exclusively.

The questions that can be asked from a wider landscape study will be different from those relating to the site locale. Fundamentally, the questions are likely to relate to the relationships between numerous sites rather that just the site in its local context. However, this will be in part determined by the type of site. For example, a linear site such as a routeway, road or cursus will necessitate a wider consideration than a more focused type of site. The direct questions relating to the site might include themes such as distribution patterns, territorial considerations or site location analyses. These are discussed below.

ANALYSING DISTRIBUTION

Site distribution is one of the earliest methodological approaches used by archaeologists (e.g. Childe 1925). Distribution may be considered at a number of different spatial resolutions, depending upon the questions being asked. This approach was used to define 'cultures' based upon distinctive assemblages of artefacts and monuments and to explore how people and ideas might have moved across Europe at different times. Whilst such approaches are based on cartographic analysis and can be conveniently addressed within the GIS, the functionality of the software enables much more complex analyses to be performed.

At a two-dimensional level distribution patterns may be addressed from the perspective of distance to certain resources, such as rivers. Using buffering algorithms, it is possible to calculate the numbers of sites of a given type within a given distance of a river system, for example. This is normally undertaken by creating a polyline file representing the river system, and then generating a buffer from that polyline, with the output being a raster of cells each with a value relating to its distance from the nearest river. This type of analysis can equally be performed in relation to other resources, and possibly used in conjunction to address themes of resource accessibility, although this is addressed in more detail below.

Similarly, distribution patterns may be addressed in a more quantitative way by looking at spatial relationships, such as through the generation of Thiessen polygons. This method effectively considers a distribution of sites as point files and calculates lines between them which can be subdivided into two. By connecting these mid-points between sites it is possible to create polygons which tentatively reflect potential territories relating to each site. This type of approach was popular during the 1970s with the development of the New Archaeology (Clarke 1978), and has been criticised for not taking other themes into account, being overly quantitative (see Johnson 1999). However, such an approach does have the potential for defining areas where sites might not have been discovered on the basis of very large 'territories'.

TERRITORIES AND VIEWSHEDS

Within analytical studies of archaeological landscapes, visibility functions within GIS have been used to address issues relating to the distribution of sites, particularly in relation to themes of territory and influence. For example, Lock and Harris (1996) demonstrated that viewsheds could be used to demonstrate socio-political units in a more useful way than Thiessen polygons. They studied the distribution of Neolithic long barrows within the Danebury landscape and found that the resulting viewshed images demonstrate very little overlap. Within this study, viewsheds were also shown to demonstrate the defensive prospect of hillforts within the region, but the authors noted that they were more importantly positioned to maximise visual dominance over valleys and other smaller settlements. Similarly, visual relationships formed the basis of conclusions made by Gaffney and Stančič (1991) about the siting of Roman towers. A slightly more complex approach by Fisher *et al.* (1997) demonstrated how viewshed analysis could be enhanced by statistical analysis of the results. In a study of Bronze Age cairns on Mull it was shown that it was possible to use viewshed analysis within a hypothesis-testing environment such that analyses may be question-led. However, the widespread use of visibility analysis within landscape interpretation has been criticised. Lake *et al.* (1998), for example, argued that the fact that intervisibility may be demonstrated between two locations may not be considered to be a reason for the location of one of the two points without analysis of other areas that may also provide the same results. Similarly, Wheatley (1996) highlighted that the results from any single analysis, such as line of sight, may only be significant relative to themselves and that other variables from other analyses may be a 'causal factor'.

Wheatley and Gillings (2000) summarised many of the criticisms of visibility analysis. This work highlighted the main limitations and critiques of the approach using three categories: pragmatic, procedural and theoretical critiques. Pragmatic critiques covered issues such as environmental factors, eyesight, mobility, simplification and causation. These critiques covered the practical problems and oversights that underlie visual analysis. Procedural critiques reflected Marozas and Zack's *operational* error (1990), reflecting upon those problems encountered through the method. Listed items included problems with the DEM, viewshed algorithms, the binary nature of viewsheds and overall robustness. They also added the concept of the 'edge effect' highlighting the problem of viewsheds that often extend beyond the edges of the DEM, or the influence of viewsheds from outside of the DEM that have the potential to extend onto it. Finally, theoretical critiques highlighted further problems. These included elements such as the 'unquestioned primacy' placed upon vision above other sensory factors, and the abstracting nature of technological determinism and, particularly, the way in which viewsheds are generally presented in plan.

The need for a qualitative approach to viewshed analysis was argued in response to these limitations. Wheatley and Gillings (2000) proposed an approach to viewsheds using a 'Higuchi' model. This classified three depths of vision, along with a range of other physical and social characteristics. It was argued that short, middle and long distance views would be relevant for different perceptual experiences and may therefore be more useful in interpretative studies.

An additional level of GIS-based visibility functionality has been termed 'multiple-viewshed analysis' (Wheatley 1995), whereby the viewsheds from multiple positions are considered together. This method was first introduced in order to investigate how intervisibility would be used within archaeology in a more robust way, particularly in the context of unknown environmental factors that could influence and restrict visibility. By generating a binary grid representing each viewshed and adding these together for each of the long barrows within his study area, it was possible to understand whether their locations displayed exceptional intervisibility. A similar study by Lock and Harris (1996) explored the relationship between different monuments within the Danebury landscape. This study demonstrated a lack of overlap from multiple viewsheds derived from the positions of long barrows in the area. This lack of overlap was interpreted to indicate that they acted as highly-visible markers defining territories. Ruggles *et al.* (1993) used a method of cumulative viewsheds, in conjunction with other tools, as a basis for generating deterministic and predictive models in relation to the locations of stone rows in northern Mull, Scotland. These models were then used to determine significant visual foci (particularly in terms of astronomical alignments) and predictively to highlight areas where other stone rows may be found.

Interpreting the purpose of cursus monuments provides a useful illustration of the use of visibility analyses using GIS. The function of Neolithic cursus monuments may be considered as an enigma, given their length, with numerous possible interpretations being posited from astronomical function (Penny and Wood 1973) to the original concept of race track (*cf.* Chippendale 1996). An analysis of the cursus complex at Rudston, East Yorkshire, showed one of the cursuses to be different from the other three, having a 'dog-leg' bend. Cumulative viewshed analysis of this monument highlighted a number of themes that assisted in its interpretation (Chapman 2003). The cumulative viewshed demonstrated a constant horizon view of two long barrows to the west; monuments that predate the construction of the cursuses and which appeared to form the focus for the architecture of the site, maintaining a link with the earlier landscape defined by the burial monuments (*34*).

MODELLING ARCHAEOLOGICAL SITE LOCATIONS

The archaeological record is both finite and incomplete. Traditionally approaches to studying landscapes and larger areas have focused on the distribution of sites or artefacts as a way of assessing trends in past activity. In a quantitative sense, this type of approach is hard to deal with as the results are determined through variable quantities of fieldwork and investigation in different areas. In some cases, large areas have not been studied and so the pattern of activity at different periods cannot be established. Despite these limitations within the archaeological record, it is sometimes appropriate to consider the wider archaeological landscape in such uninvestigated areas, for a number of reasons. A development such as large-scale forestry might pose a threat to the unknown archaeological resource of an area. Forestry can cover expansive areas which would make traditional fieldwork-based mitigation inappropriate or prohibitively expensive, particularly given the unknown nature of the resource. In such cases it can be advantageous to undertake targeted fieldwork based upon models simulating the most probable locations of archaeological sites in comparison to more comprehensively studied areas. In these cases, GIS can provide a point of departure by generating predictive models displaying areas of greater or lesser archaeological potential.

It is often possible to postulate trends in archaeological data. For example, it might be observed that many prehistoric occupation sites in a given area lie on south-facing slopes, presumably to take maximum advantage of the sun. The same might be said for field systems. There might also be resource implications; the proximity of most sites to a water source, for example. Similarly, Roman-period cemeteries might normally be associated with contemporary roads. The generalisations of trends in the archaeological data in relation to environmental and cultural information are widespread. On the basis of such trends, it is possible to begin to model where certain sites are more or less likely to be.

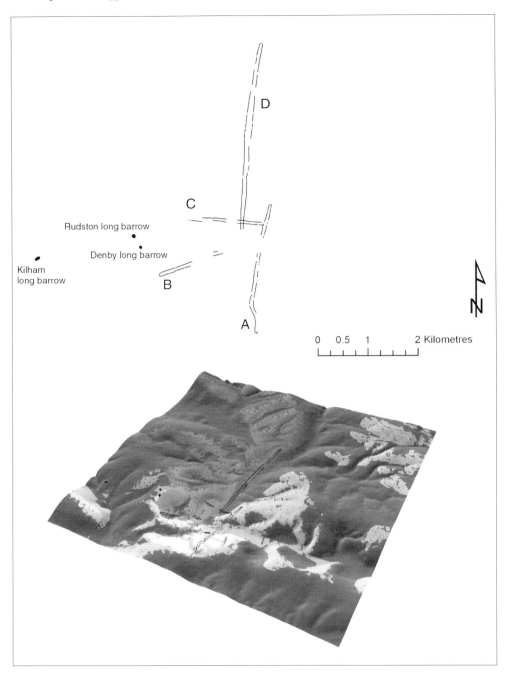

34 Cumulative viewshed model of the Rudston landscape, East Yorkshire, showing the areas (in lighter shades) which would be most frequently seen whilst moving along cursus A. It may be noted that the Rudston and Denby long barrows maintain a view on the western horizon during this route, perhaps indicating a reason for the 'dog-leg' in the plan of the cursus

Before continuing with examples, there has been much debate on the efficacy of using such generalisations, particularly when considering cultural activity in the past. The environmental determinism debate (*cf.* Gaffney and van Leusen 1995) has been prevalent in relation to GIS-based predictive modelling. To what extent are the activities of people in the past determined by their environment? It can be postulated that the interpretations of activities during different periods have been more or less environmentally determined than during others. To quote Bradley:

> in the literature as a whole, successful farmers have social relations with one another, while hunter-gatherers have ecological relations with hazelnuts (Bradley 1984, 11).

Much has been written about the predictive modelling of archaeological site locations using GIS. The approach has proven popular in areas of the United States and continental Europe, although it has been less well used within the UK. To take an example of this type of work, areas of middle-late Bronze Age agriculture in an upland environment may be considered (*colour plate 8*). Observed examples have demonstrated a number of consistent themes. We can say that in each of the observed cases, there has been a correlation between field systems and the reuse of early Bronze Age barrows, and that this link has been firstly visual and secondly proximal. Thirdly, in each case, field systems have been found on south-facing slopes, being advantageous in terms of climate. Fourthly, the field systems have been on gentle gradients where soil depletion is likely to be less pronounced. In terms of the GIS, models may be erected of each of these situations. Barrow visibility can be understood in terms of a viewshed model, and proximity through a distance buffer. South-facing slopes may be calculated using an aspect function, and a slope model will provide information regarding gradient. If models are generated for each of these scenarios the results will consist of four different GIS rasters.

1. *Viewshed.* This is a binary model whereby cells in the raster are ascribed a 1 for visible areas and a 0 for invisible areas from the barrow.
2. *Distance.* This model outputs cells relating to distance from the barrow.
3. *Aspect.* The resulting aspect model provides cell values in degrees from 0–360 reflecting the compass direction that any slopes are facing. Flat areas at given a value of –1.
4. *Slope.* Slope can be calculated in terms of degrees, giving cell values between 0 and 90, or per cent, giving values of between 0 and 100.

In their raw form, these models provide qualitative information for assessing site locations, such as perhaps demonstrating that most known settlements of a given period might be located on south-facing slopes. However, the different values of each of the resulting models (e.g. slope measured between 0 and 90 degrees, and aspect measuring between 0 and 360 degrees) mean that multiple surface analyses are less meaningful. Instead, each model needs to be calibrated to enable the correct weighting of each to the study. As it stands in this example, there is the assumption, on the basis of the observed phenomena, that each of the four parameters is of equal importance. Thus, if each of the models is reclassified to reflect equal weighting on the basis of the information that is required, it becomes possible to begin a more quantitative analysis. Viewshed already provides binary values of appropriate areas (visible, or 1) and inappropriate areas (not visible, or 0). Using this as a basis, it is possible to reclassify the other themes on the same basis, with a value of 1 for suitable areas and 0 for unsuitable areas. Aspect may be considered as suitable when areas are either flat (cell value –1), or broadly face south (90-270 degrees), and so the model may be recalibrated with these areas becoming 1 and all other areas becoming 0. Similarly, slope may be reclassified. Arbitrarily, a value can be chosen for slope beyond which it becomes too steep for agriculture. This may be obtained from the observed archaeological remains in the field. For example, it might be decided that 0-5 degrees may be classified as suitable and given a value of 1, whereby greater slopes may be unsuitable and given a value of 0. Without considering distance for the time being, these three binary models may be considered together. By adding the three models together, the resulting calculation will return a raster with cell values ranging from 0-3, where the higher the number, the higher the potential for finding Bronze Age field remains, within the parameters being modelled. In terms of distance, it is possible either to assess this qualitatively from the resulting model, or else provide a level of 'fuzziness'. In reclassifying the distance model, there are a number of options. We can either generate a binary model based upon observed data for the maximum distance from a barrow that field systems have been recorded, or else it can be assumed that the closer to the barrow the better. In the latter case, the values for the reclassification of the distance model might range linearly between 1 for the closest areas and 0 for areas further away, providing fractions for cells in between. The advantage of this type of model is that it is less prescriptive and allows for the modelling of trends rather than absolutes. By adding the resulting reclassified distance model to the other three models, 4 becomes the most suitable area, but with a more gradual distribution of less suitable areas. Equally, fuzzy reclassifications can be used for the other parameters such as slope and aspect, where the most suitable areas are provided with the highest values, but where there is a graduation between this and the unsuitable areas. This type of modelling enables us to begin considering the unknown data which are all appropriate for archaeology.

In addition to approaching site location analysis from a fuzzy modelling perspective, it is also sometimes appropriate to add weighting to different models. For example, it might be considered that visibility is more important than the other factors in setting out where field systems would be, and so its values for suitable areas could be 2 rather than 1, doubling its weighting in the resulting model. Ultimately, these values may be tweaked to provide a best fit to observed data and from that it becomes possible to extrapolate the model to wider areas. However, it should be remembered that GIS only provides a model and that this model is only as good as the input data and the ways in which those data are managed. Thus such a GIS model should be considered as a guide to fieldwork, and also something that needs to be tested, including the testing of areas that have not been predicted in order to limit criticisms of determinism. Otherwise, the results may be tested in other ways within the GIS. By excluding parts of the archaeological data at the outset, models can be made using the data that are left. Once a best fit model has been generated, it can be tested against the data that were excluded.

Due to the nature of such models, and also to the themes of determinism, the use of predictive modelling has been the subject of much debate. Much of this has been within its role in cultural resource management (CRM), and will be considered in chapter 10.

MODELLING ROUTEWAYS

Another aspect of GIS functionality is the capability of modelling routeways of 'least-cost', frequently referred to as cost-path analysis. On a flat, uniform landscape, the easiest or fastest route between two points will normally be a straight line. In a GIS, this flat surface may be represented as a raster, whereby the 'cost' of the route will be determined by adding the values of all cells which the route passes through together. If each cell has a value of 1, then the total cost will be $1+1+1+1n$. Hence, a longer distance will have a greater cost compared with a shorter route. In more hilly terrain, slope might be considered to be costly in terms of movement. A steep slope will clearly have a greater cost to movement than a flat area. In this case, the raster will have higher cell values for areas of steeper slope compared with those areas of more gentle gradients. Any route through the landscape may be considered as the total of all cells passed through between two points. Hence the costs (in cell values) of any route through the landscape between two points can be calculated. Furthermore, it is possible to use the GIS to generate the 'least–cost route' by identifying the pathway which incurs the least cumulative values in relation to the cost-surface model.

Cost of moving through an archaeological landscape is a subjective concept and may apply to a number of parameters. Whilst slope might be important, areas of bog, rivers and other physical barriers may be ascribed values within a raster relating to cost of movement through them. Similarly, conceptual boundaries to movement might include foreign territories or sacred areas; 'Topography is a fundamental component of the mechanics of movement and yet is by no means the complete explanation of it' (Bell and Lock 2000, 88). Whilst the GIS interpretation of least-cost paths is algorithmic, it is entirely dependent upon the user's definition of the cost-surface and which factors they consider to be of greatest importance. In the traditional model, however, the principal factor used in the construction of cost-surfaces has been slope. For example, Gaffney and Stančič (1991) interpreted the general accessibility of the landscape of the island of Hvar, Croatia, on the basis of cost-path analysis, with cost being defined by slope. More complex approaches have incorporated considerations of slope in relation to other factors. Madry and Rakos (1996), for example, examined routes between hillforts on the basis of slope in conjunction with maintaining highest possible elevation and maximum view of hillforts in the area. However, regardless of the influence of other factors, some consideration of the caveats of slope-based cost-surface modelling should be made. Principally, there are two themes to consider:

Slope angle and cost
Traditional approaches to defining cost-surfaces based on slope have considered increase of slope as having a constant relationship to increase in effort. The slope model defines a raster based upon an elevation raster, or DEM, whereby cell values are calculated as the maximum rate of change between a cell and its eight neighbours, and can be expressed in degrees or percentage. If the slope model provides raster cell values between 1° and 60°, and is used as the cost-surface, then effort is assumed to be 60 times greater for the steepest slopes compared with the flatter areas. However, in practice things are more complex. Effort may be defined as a function of the mass of the person walking, the gravitational pull on that person and the height ascended over a given horizontal distance. As the first two factors, mass and gravity, are constant, then the only variable in defining effort is change in elevation. Effectively this means that any increase in the angle of slope reflects a greater change in elevation between starting point and finishing point. The traditional slope model only provides values relating to slope change and not effort, since it does not take elevation into account, but only angles of slope. A way of getting round this and generating an accurate model of

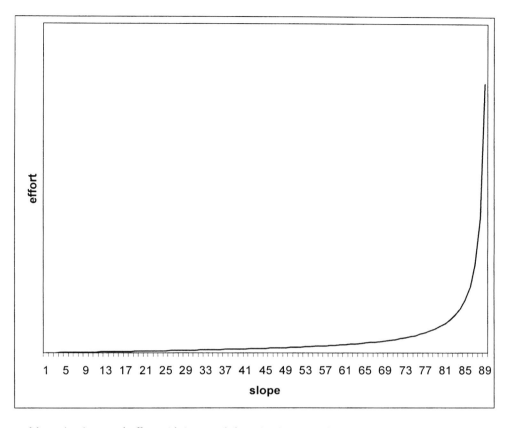

35 Measuring increased effort with increased slope (in degrees) when moving through a landscape using the algorithm defined by Bell and Lock (2000)

effort in the cost–surface has been proposed by Bell and Lock (2000) through the use of trigonometry. If the resulting surface is to reflect effort, it is calculated for movement between each cell, providing a known distance for each calculation, defined by the cell size of the raster. The difference in effort between climbing a gentle slope (A) compared with a steep slope (B) over the same horizontal distance (each cell) can be expressed from the slope model angles as *tanA : tanB*. This provides understanding of shift in elevation between the two cells (35). To take the example of the earlier slope model with values ranging between 1° and 60°, using the tangent calibration, effort values defined in cells will be between 0.01745–1.7320. Hence it becomes 99 times more effort to climb a 60° slope compared with a slope of just 1°.

Direction of movement

The second issue relating to using slope as a cost-surface for pathway analysis lies with the direction of movement. Fundamentally, slope will provide impedance against movement uphill, but will provide little resistance to someone moving downhill. Thus the direction in which someone moves will influence the amount of effort that is required. In some cases, movement downhill will reduce the cost of travel to the person moving through the landscape. In terms of many routeways that function in both directions this will clearly be less of an issue. However, when interpreting routes through a landscape with an element of directionality, further calibration is required. In these cases an anisotropic cost algorithm may be used (Bell and Lock 2000, De Silva and Pizziolo 2001). This algorithm incorporates the direction of force (i.e. downslope) in conjunction with its magnitude (slope). Effectively, an anisotropic algorithm will imply force against someone moving uphill and force with someone moving downhill. Whilst this is appropriate for most applications, there is no consideration of the implications of this over very rough terrain. Beyond certain thresholds in slope, effort moving downhill will ultimately become increased as the slope no longer assists movement.

In an archaeological sense, analysing routeways becomes important for a number of reasons and this has been demonstrated in a variety of cases. For example, a consideration of hillfort positions on the prehistoric Ridgeway in Oxfordshire prompted researchers to interpret an early date for its origins (Bell and Lock 2000). The results from cost-path analysis demonstrated that the prehistoric Ridgeway deviated in places from its modern position, in some cases passing though the centre of hillforts. This implied that a function of the hillforts may have been to control movement along the Ridgeway. Hillforts were positioned to control movement along the route at the expense of maintaining long-distance visibility of the landscape, calculated using viewed analysis. The implications of this work were that the Ridgeway predated the construction of the hillforts along the route, which appeared to serve a particular function.

A simple example of the archaeological application of cost-path analysis using GIS is through the study of Roman roads in Bath (*colour plate 9*). In this area, a series of excavations and observations have recorded sections of Roman-period roads within the modern city in areas that would have been outside of the Roman-period urban limits. Whilst the positions of the roads approaching Bath are quite well known, where these roads pass between the observed sections is not. Greater significance in terms of the roads may be placed in relation to other Roman-period activities in the surrounding landscape, including villas and associated cemeteries. Hence, through a greater understanding of the roads surrounding Roman Bath, it would be possible to interpret the wider contemporary landscape. In this case it was possible to firstly assess the positions of known roads within the landscape to consider to what extent their positions were determined by topographic variables. By generating different 'cost-surfaces' based on variations in the weighting of different factors (including slope) it was possible to compare the routes of different 'least-cost paths' with the known positions of the roads. On the basis of this work it was possible to extrapolate by using the best-fit cost-surface to determine the least-cost route through the areas where the position of the road is not known. Using the ends of the known (excavated) sections of road as starting and finishing positions, it was possible to extrapolate a predicted routeway that best fitted the parameters defined by the raster. This effectively filled in the gaps in the Roman road pattern, with hypothetical road positions which could be tested through future fieldwork.

CONCLUSIONS

In this chapter the ways in which GIS can address the types of questions that are common within landscape analysis have been considered. This has involved a range of functions including map overlay and vector-based modelling. In addition, other ways of modelling archaeological situations on the basis of observed data have been considered as well as methods of extrapolating it for areas where data are less available. This has been demonstrated in relation to viewshed analysis, site location analysis and the defining of routeways through cost–path analysis. It has also shown that, whilst single methods of analysis can be used to address certain singular questions, the use of multiple approaches together can generate more sophisticated models that can ultimately focus fieldwork for further investigation. In the next chapter, themes of predictive modelling are considered further, but in relation to the modelling of past physical landscapes, and particularly the reconstruction of environmental changes.

7

Landscape archaeology as reconstruction

INTRODUCTION

In the previous chapter the ways in which GIS can be used to strip away more recent layers of human activity to reveal earlier ones, to analyse observable data, and to predict the positions of archaeological features through the extrapolation of identified trends and phenomena were explored. A substantial element of understanding archaeological landscapes involves the interpretation of what landscape features were in the area at a given time (*colour plate 10*). In addition to the archaeological landscape, it is important to consider what the natural environment might have been like. This might have impacts on the activities of people, or might have been impacted upon by people in the past. To quote Mark Gillings to:

> attempt to examine the organisation of activity foci in the context of the surrounding landscape requires that the following fundamental assumption to hold true. The modern observable landscape form, and its related dynamics must be closely comparable to those in operation during antiquity (Gillings 1995, 67).

Hence, a consideration of the environment remains important. Furthermore, GIS provides the format to put some flesh on the bones of environmental archaeology through the reconstruction of environmental factors, including presenting a forum for examining and modelling issues such as the rate of change. However, there is some room for caution here. The use of GIS within archaeology has been accused of being environmentally deterministic (see Gaffney and van Leusen 1995) due to the reliance on the interpretation of the interaction between environmental factors and cultural activity. Within the realms of palaeoenvironmental reconstruction, particularly where it is linked with the interpretation of cultural landscapes and people's activities in the past, users of GIS should arguably be sympathetic to this debate.

PALAEOENVIRONMENTAL DATA

Landscapes change through time. On the surface, elements of vegetation change. The most significant events might be considered to be the early post-glacial period with the establishment of pine and birch forest in many areas, or perhaps woodland clearance. At a deeper level, changes to sea level will alter how the lowlands and river valleys appear and react significantly, with changes such as alluviation, peat growth (*36*) and alterations to the nature of the channel itself; its width and speed of flow. In some areas changes in climate have resulted in massive landscape changes, such as the growth of blanket peat over areas of upland moorland. Raised bogs will have seen dramatic change with the development of wet fen to ombrotrophic peat, killing other forms of vegetation as conditions become wetter and more acidic. In some cases environmental change can be extremely rapid, particularly with relation to catastrophic events, whilst in other cases change is more gradual. The potential to model rate of change is also within the toolkit provided by GIS.

The importance of integrating palaeoenvironmental data into landscape studies has been demonstrated on numerous occasions. In a paper produced in 1997 Bender, Tilley and Hamilton examined a broad range of factors relating to a Bronze Age landscape near Leskernick on Bodmin Moor, Cornwall (Bender *et al.* 1997). Many considerations were made, and some very new and innovative ideas and methods were presented. Within the investigation of the site, the views from each of the 'huts' were examined through the construction of a portable wooden door frame that could be positioned so that the views from inside the dwellings during the Bronze Age could be reconstructed. A number of theories were generated from this exercise about significant places outside of the settlement. However, recent research in the area had investigated the palaeoecology of the area and specifically the types of vegetation that would have been present at the time that the settlement was occupied (Gearey *et al.* 2000a, 2000b). The results from this research had demonstrated that the landscape at that time was dominated by dense hazel woodland. This would most clearly have obscured and altered the view from the settlement, when compared with that of today, and raised a number of new questions. Fundamentally, if those views were so important during the Bronze Age then they would have needed to be maintained. Otherwise the view theory would need to be discredited. At one

36 Hatfield Moors, South Yorkshire. This wetland landscape conceals a later Neolithic landscape buried beneath peat following extreme environmental change over the past 5000 years

level, it is not possible to know where each tree would have been within the landscape, but through considering the impact of palaeoenvironmental data it becomes possible to begin altering the types of theories and interpretations that may be delivered (Chapman and Gearey 2000).

Palaeoenvironmental data come in a number of different formats. These include the results from traditional scientific approaches, such as pollen, plant macrofossils and insects, and also evidence from historical maps, textual descriptions and intuitive approaches. Scientific approaches, such as palynology, normally result in diagrams indicating changes in vegetation communities by depth. Sometimes these diagrams will have radiocarbon dates associated with particular layers. Pollen diagrams are commonly expressed as statistical representations of species as a percentage of total land pollen. There are numerous considerations to be made when interpreting pollen diagrams, including the relative quantity of pollen produced by different species, its dispersal distance (Birks and Birks 1980) and differential decay in the soil (Havinga 1984). It is also important to consider the different types of ecological conditions that different species require. However, for the purposes of modelling, the level of detail should be considered in relation to the questions being asked of the landscape and the spatial resolution at which analyses are being made. Other types of palaeoenvironmental data include the quantities and types of molluscs, insects and plant macrofossils within a sedimentary unit which can each provide different levels of information about different environments and at different spatial scales, although it is normally best to consider multiple sources of data to provide an overview of the landscape at a particular time. In addition, microfossils from diatoms can provide information on salinity of an environment at a particular time and testate amoebae can provide information regarding surface wetness at a specific level. A consideration of different forms of data in relation to date and vertical position can also provide information regarding sea level at a given period (e.g. Long *et al.* 1998). As a rule, the more layers of palaeoenvironmental data that are available, the better for understanding the past environment.

Other forms of data include historical documents including maps and textual descriptions of the environment. As mentioned in chapter 4, these sources can provide a range of information regarding how an environment appeared at a particular time, although these are arguably more useful for more recent periods and might be more comprehensive for some geographical areas than others.

Intuitive approaches might seem less relevant but do have some applicability here, particularly in cases where other data do not exist. For example, in the case of industrial archaeological sites, woodland might be considered to be of importance as one of many resources needed to keep the machinery running. We might know that dense woodland existed, but not its exact location. Some indication will be available from a consideration of where woodland remains today and an investigation of these areas on the ground might give a better indication (e.g. Muir 2000). However, it is normally likely that much of the woodland will have since been cleared. In a hypothetical sense, it becomes possible to model areas more likely to have been woodland; the steeper valley slopes perhaps and other areas which might not have been used for other functions. Whatever the case, hypothetical modelling of these areas can be useful in beginning to interpret the landscape in a more holistic sense.

VEGETATION MODELLING

Mapping vegetation within a GIS is most appropriately achieved through ascribing polygons to different vegetation types, whether these relate to single tree types or, more usually, to vegetation communities. Previously, studies aimed at reconstructing patterns of vegetation have been approached from a number of angles. The most obvious position for generating a GIS model of vegetation, particularly in the absence of palaeoenvironmental data, is through the intuitive modelling of trees on steeper slopes of a landscape. It may be considered that the steeper slopes will be the last areas to be cleared of woodland. In the absence of a clear opportunity for arable cultivation, these areas of the landscape could be profitably utilised for managed woodland and perhaps woodland grazing. Whilst it might not always be the case, in the absence of other forms of data, it is reasonable to assume that areas of woodland might persist on valley slopes for longer than elsewhere. Having assumed this, it becomes possible to generate a model of what the landscape might have looked like at a particular period, based on this single hypothesis. In terms of GIS, normally only topography is considered and, in particular, the differences in slope. To perform this analysis, it is necessary to obtain a DEM of the area of study. This provides us with a raster model where each cell's attributes relate to elevation. Assuming that the area of study is topographically variable, with large variations in elevation, it becomes appropriate to investigate slope. Within most GIS packages there is a function whereby it is possible to derive slope from the DEM (see chapter 5). This calculation assesses the difference in height between adjacent cells within the DEM to generate a new raster where each cell relates to slope angle or per cent. In the resulting raster, higher cell values will relate to greater slope. Thus, it becomes possible to bracket steeper slopes from flatter areas. The exact values for this might be subjectively selected and dependent upon the topography of the area of study. From this it becomes possible to either reassign values for the raster (steep slopes = 1, other areas = 0) or else to use the appropriate grid or raster calculator to generate polygons of those areas where steep slopes are encountered. Either way, the output provides a visual representation of where the wooded valleys are most likely to have been within the landscape, and at the very least provides a hypothetical model that might be tested and adapted through additional research (*colour plate 11*).

Taking things further, it is possible to model past vegetation patterns based on a mixture of input data, including slope, elevation, soil type, geology and so forth. Spikins (2000) presented an interpretative vegetation map for the north of England using a combination of input variables. It was considered that, within a given context, plant communities within a landscape could be predicted. Input variables were substrate type (with soil types categorised into six principal groups based on geology), altitudinal limits (in relation to climate, with data obtained from beetle analyses, and contours being used to examine lines of maximum tree growth at different times of climate change following the last Ice Age), coastlines (interpreted for sea–level change and isostatic uplift, used within the GIS as a series of dated outlines, providing more of an aesthetic function rather than being involved in the analysis) and tree spread for different species (using Birks' (1989) model of tree spread in 500-year time slices following the last glaciation).

Each of the input–data layers were generated as vector polygons. By combining the layers, many smaller polygons were created, being the union of each of the input variables, constructed from elevation (calculated at 50m interval bands), soils and tree spread (changing for each time slice of 500 years). An algorithm was then written to define the most likely dominant tree type within each of these smaller polygons through an assessment of each tree species in relation to other parameters within the model. The results were rendered using the dominant species attribute for each of the polygons at each of the time-slice periods. The study covered the whole of the north of England, north of the Wash, and so a low resolution was appropriate.

At a higher resolution, and incorporating a more comprehensive interpretation of pollen data, a study of an Iron Age wetland landscape at Sutton Common, South Yorkshire, was made possible through the modelling of a single plant type that was abundant within the contemporaneous palynological record (Gearey and Chapman 2005). The plant was *Alnus* (alder), which displays a number of ecological preferences. Alder can grow in wet areas where water levels do not exceed certain heights. Essentially they like their roots seasonally wet, but not too wet. Within the area of study, a number of additional sources of data already existed from other research. These included water table data, providing the modern shape of the water table and its seasonal fluctuations over the local area. Through a consideration of the levels of archaeological and palaeoenvironmental deposits it was possible to provide an approximation of likely levels of the water table across the site during the Iron Age. Through modelling the water table in relation to the ground surface, it was possible to indicate where the water was in relation to the ground surface – above it or below it, and to what extent. With the prevalence of alder within the pollen layers contemporary with the Iron Age features it was considered that the reconstruction of a single species was appropriate. Using this model it was possible to classify areas of the appropriate levels of wetness and to reconstruct alder vegetation (*37*).

Given the strict groundwater conditions in which alder will grow naturally, it was possible to reconstruct areas of the DEM that were wet enough, but not too wet. Subtracting the DEM from the water table raster, cell values provide information of distance of the water surface from the ground surface, with positive values reflecting standing water and negative values reflecting groundwater. This was also achieved using a constrained random cell-generator with values of between zero and eight, reflecting the range in height of typical alder carr. In this case, areas of standing water could also be modelled. The results from the modelling included areas of carr within an area of the archaeological enclosure and across the top of a causeway leading to the site. It seemed unlikely that carr would have been growing on the areas that were being constructed at that time and so a level of 'gardening' was carried out.

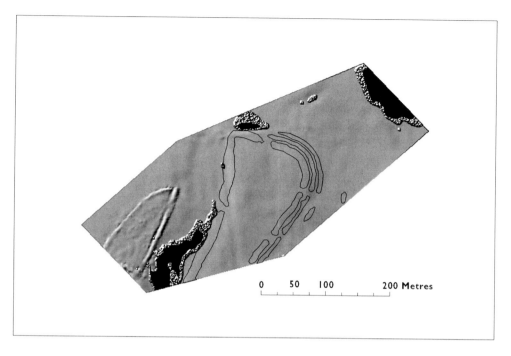

37 Hillshaded DEM of Sutton Common with reconstructed alder carr vegetation and standing water

A range of other approaches are currently being developed to accurately model vegetation from palaeoenvironmental data. For example, one approach has been to generate models from modern pollen assemblages where the vegetation pattern may be measured (e.g. Fyfe 2006). Fundamentally, however, within a GIS, the representation of vegetation can be troublesome. For example, the modelling of tree patterns has been undertaken as polygon blocks which inhibit the true nature of vegetation in terms of movement or visibility through it (Tschan *et al.* 2000).

MODELLING ENVIRONMENTAL CHANGE

Whilst vegetation is clearly important, depending on the time frame which is being considered, the modelling of geomorphological change can be extremely important. For example, large landscape change, such as through river movements, flooding (e.g. Gillings 1995), erosion (e.g. Verhagen 1996), sediment movement (e.g. Wainwright and Thornes 1991) or peat growth, can alter the nature of the landscape considerably and thus influence the way in which the archaeology of palaeo-landscapes is interpreted. Within inland areas this is normally most dramatic in the case of rivers, with the masking, land-altering consequences of alleviation, particularly as a consequence of sea-level changes (see Long *et al.* 1998). Within the Upper Tisza Valley in north-east Hungary, a study attempted to address the issue of fluvial activity, and particularly flooding, in relation to cultural activity (Gillings 1995). This study integrated a combination of topographic parameters (elevation) with hydrological functions within the GIS and proximity to water sources (rivers) and borehole data to simulate a flood event in the past. It was recognised that elevation alone was insufficient to simulate the effects of flooding and that proximity to the river was also important. Furthermore, the complexities of water run-off and movement over the surface of a landscape will affect the impact of a flood event on a community in the past. The results of this study demonstrated, for example, that the cycles of flooding within the Upper Tisza Valley had a 'marked impact upon the settlement and exploitation of the region during the Middle Neolithic' (Gillings 1995, 82). In this case it was concluded that the value of GIS could 'not be over-stressed' in creating a more robust analysis of the archaeological remains in the area (*Ibid.* 83).

A second dramatic environmental change which can significantly alter an environment through time, and in contrast to alluviation and flooding, is the development of peat bogs which can mask earlier landscapes, both within uplands and lowlands. However, the most dramatic of such cases are within lowland raised mires. Here, regional environmental changes, such as increases in sea level, can result in an increase in the surface wetness of an area, initially leading to shifts in local vegetation which will inevitably have an influence on cultural activity. In the case of raised mires, these developing wetlands are transformed, resulting in peat growth as the processes of organic break down of dead vegetation is inhibited by the raised water table and consequently anoxic conditions (Coles and Coles 1996, Van de Noort *et al.* 2001, Chapman and Cheetham 2002). With the dead vegetation not rotting, and the continued growth of additional species such as *Sphagnum* mosses, the developing mire surface becomes divorced from the local hydrology and grows, thus becoming 'raised' and hydrologically fed by precipitation alone.

From a cultural archaeological perspective, the significance of raised mires may be split into two principal themes. The first is defined by the exceptional preservation of organic material, including bog bodies (e.g. Globb 1998, Turner and Scaife 1995), within them. The second has more significance to the landscape archaeologist. The tremendous changes to such a landscape provide some exceptional challenges to interpretation. The changes themselves, often from dryland to wetland through to raised mire, present both physical changes and changes in the way that a landscape may be exploited. Through the growth of the mire surface, the original land surface becomes impossible to read as a landscape from any single period. Shifts in both space (three-dimensional) and time make the interpretation of archaeological sites, and the prediction of the locations of other possible sites in these landscapes very difficult. This situation is extremely frustrating given the exceptional preservation potential that they hold and the threat of ongoing commercial peat cutting that persists on many of these sites.

The palaeoenvironmental complexity of these landscapes means that they cannot be readily interpreted on the ground. Hence, GIS-based approaches to landscape reconstruction and visualisation become extremely relevant. The raised mires of Thorne and Hatfield Moors in South Yorkshire are the two largest lowland peat bogs in the UK, measuring 5.5 x 5.5km and 4.6 x 4.8km respectively. A GIS-based approach to interpreting the environmental development of these landscapes has been developed to provide a basis for interpreting and predicting archaeological site locations within them (Chapman and Gearey 2003). Here the process was based upon the creation of a pre-peat land surface (*38*), based on a variety of data sources including borehole data and geophysical survey (Ground Penetrating Radar (GPR)).

The reconstruction of the pre-peat landscape presents an early dryland landscape that could be interpreted as any other. Hence, the possible locations of archaeological sites within such a landscape can thus be predicted in relation to the regional picture (in this case provided by Van de Noort and Ellis 1997). Through the GIS-based integration of the results from stratigraphic and palaeoenvironmental

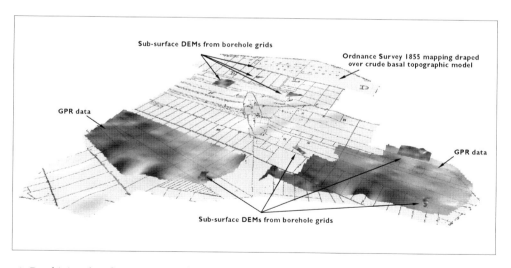

38 Combining data from a variety of sources to build up an understanding of past landscapes – Hatfield Moors, South Yorkshire (4.5 x 4.5km looking from the south)

analyses (e.g. pollen, testate amoebae and coleopteran, particularly from previous studies), in conjunction with various dating methods, the growth of the mire at different periods can be modelled in relation to the initial pre-peat surface providing time–slice mapping for different periods. From this position, through the creation of a four-dimensional model of the development of the mire, it becomes possible to begin applying more standard landscape archaeology approaches to the interpretation of the landscape at different periods.

MODELLING THE SEA

One of the more dramatic changes to a landscape can be due to changes in sea level. This can have a direct impact, such as the flooding of the North Sea basin during the early Holocene, or an indirect impact such as isostatic changes. For areas where shifts in sea level have been significant it is impossible to begin to interpret landscapes without a high level of reconstruction, whether this is conceptually, physically or digitally. As the GIS provides the opportunity to apply algorithms to a landscape surface, it is possible to begin retrospective modelling of landscapes based upon what is understood from the archaeological and palaeoenvironmental records.

An example of where such a reconstruction is required before a landscape may be interpreted is the site of Green Island, near Poole in Dorset (*colour plate 12*). Here an intense level of Iron Age-period industry and trade was being conducted on what is currently an island within Poole Harbour. A submerged routeway is known to have accessed the island, indicating that the water level had considerably risen in the intermediate time period. This is reflected by the palaeoenvironmental data which provides a 'sea-level curve' for the region; effectively a time/elevation graph. In this case, the archaeology within the current landscape made less sense and so it was advantageous to model how the landscape may have appeared during the Iron Age. The Ordnance Survey data provide elevations for land, but does not model the submerged landscape. Thus this data source could only be used for part of the modelling process. Bathymetric data is commonly available from organisations such as the Admiralty who produce charts for shipping. By combining bathymetric data with the Ordnance Survey Landform Profile data, it is possible to generate models combining the two. One approach to this is to create a model based on the Ordnance Survey data and to create a separate model based on the bathymetric data, whilst ensuring that areas outside of the bathymetry are provided with a value of 0 rather than 'NoData'. This ensures that calculations can be made between the two resulting models. By adding the bathymetry (which should be in negative values if calibrated to absolute heights) to the Ordnance Survey data derived surface, the resulting model should provide subsurface detail. Other forms of data may be used to clean up elements of the resulting model as required. Once this DEM has been created it becomes possible to recreate contemporary sea level for any given period by reading its height from the sea-level curve and reconstructing that as a polygon or raster over the top of it. Thus the impact of varying sea level may be examined in relation to the archaeology. In the case of Green Island, the resulting model made it possible to visualise the Iron Age environment and thus make more sense of how the site related to the surrounding landscape. However, it should also be considered that, whilst such a visualisation is clearly useful, it is also limited as it makes no consideration of river migration and more subtle geomorphological change. These can be added to the DEM as required, depending on the nature of the input data that are available.

Similarly, the inundation of the North Sea basin during the early Holocene has resulted in a large area of a prehistoric landscape being effectively unreachable archaeologically. Whilst geophysical approaches are being used to investigate this landscape (e.g. Fitch *et al.* 2005) the question of social impact of inundation may be addressed using a proxy landscape. In this case it has been suggested that a suitable analogy for the submerged landscape is that of Holderness, East Yorkshire (Coles 1998). Here it is possible to begin addressing the impact of sea-level rise. Using a DEM of the Holderness landscape in conjunction with flint scatters obtained from fieldwalking (Van de Noort and Ellis 1995) it is possible to begin investigating the rate of landscape change in relation to the rate of sea-level rise (*39*).

Whilst high-resolution data relating to sea-level change is hard to determine, a generalised model for the period from 7500-4000 cal BP (later Mesolithic to Bronze Age) has been provided by Long *et al.* (1998). They have calculated that during this time sea level in the Humber region changed from approximately -9m OD to 0m OD, a mean rise of *c.*3.9mm per year. This figure reduced gradually to *c.*1mm per year after 4000 cal BP. While the earlier figure relates to Mesolithic sea-level rise it also provides a linear basis from which to calculate inundation in relation to the proxy DEM of Holderness and thus its potential effect on contemporary populations (*40*).

In other words, it becomes possible to address whether the timescales for change would have been sufficiently short for it to have been recognised by contemporary populations. By calculating 10-year blocks (i.e. 39mm steps), the increase in surface area of water can be modelled, in addition to assessing changes in access across the landscape. The results from this study (Chapman and Lillie 2004) demonstrated that only localised change would have been discerned for the first 100 years of modelling but that, following this period, rapid inundation is shown in the model, suddenly covering large areas of the

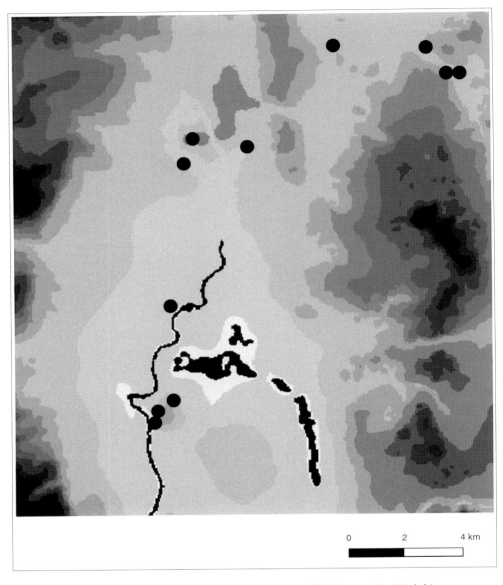

39 Above: The proxy Doggerland` landscape, using a section of Holderness, East Yorkshire

40 Opposite: Hypothetical inundation rates of the proxy Doggerland landscape following the known sea-level curve

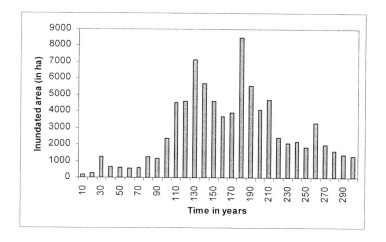

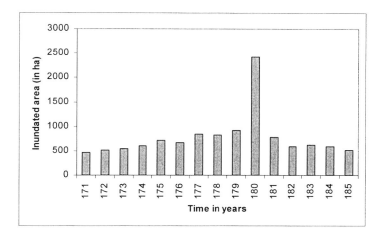

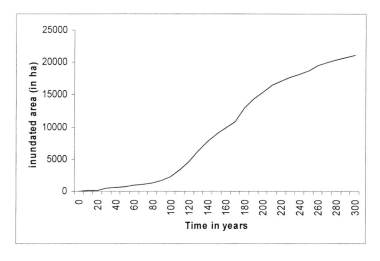

landscape. Furthermore, at certain times there were significantly greater levels of inundation whereby dramatic flooding took place over very short time periods. This is perhaps more significant insofar that, if the model is correct, this flooding would have occurred during the later Mesolithic period at which time the rate of sea level had significantly reduced. Potentially this would mean that perception of flooding might have been greater at a time when the actual rate of sea-level rise had reduced. Furthermore, the nature of the inundation would have suddenly obstructed routes through the landscape which might have had a greater conceptual effect on populations than the loss of dry landmass.

A third example of *relative* sea-level rise in relation to archaeology has been a previous study of Finland (Nunez *et al.* 1995). Finland and its neighbours were affected quite dramatically by isostatic rebound following the end of the last (Devensian) glaciation. In Finland, whilst isostatic rebound has diminished since deglaciation, the country is still rising by rates of 9mm per year in the north-west and by 3mm per year in the south-east. In contrast, during the eighth millennium BC, rates were approximately 120mm per year and 30mm per year in these same regions. As a result of this, the land area of Finland has increased over time with more rising from the Baltic Sea. To add further complication to the environmental history of the country, sea-level rise throughout the post-glacial period has been variable, at times both slower and faster than the rate of isostatic rebound, with sea-level transgressions continuing until about 6000 BC. The overall affects of this have been variable (though mostly increased) land area, a dramatically shifting shoreline, with additional effects on ecological zones, and thus resources, further inland.

This type of dramatic environmental change means that the interpretation of cultural activity through time can be extremely problematic if attempts to model them are not made. Thus the development of GIS within archaeology in some regions has been crucial. However, in terms of GIS it does present certain difficulties not least due to the tilting aspect of the landscape which varies in different areas through time. To address this Nunez *et al.* (1995) wrote an algorithm by which to simulate the topography as a DEM for any given period. Studying the area around Lake Saimaa, they calculated that ancient elevation values for a given cell within the DEM would be equal to the present elevation of that cell, minus the interpolated value for land uplift for that cell in metres per century, multiplied by time expressed in years. From the basis of this reconstruction, the distribution of archaeological sites of different periods could be placed within their simulated contemporary landscapes, thus providing additional data for interpretation.

In a similar study, the dynamic coastlines of southern Norway were modelled in order to understand the landscape archaeology of Mesolithic activity within the region (Boaz and Uleberg 2000). The results from this work highlighted how, through environmental reconstruction, it was possible to begin to interpret cultural changes based upon the contemporary landscape perception and the importance of natural places in such interpretations. Through reconstruction, the distributions of artefactual material could be analysed more appropriately and engaged with in a virtual way.

THE LIMITS OF MODELLING

There are a number of limitations to the GIS modelling of environmental conditions that should be highlighted at this juncture. Perhaps most importantly, the model is only as good as the data that it relies on. In many cases the GIS merely provides a visualisation of what those data might actually mean. Whilst this is a useful tool for understanding potentially complex datasets, GIS models should be treated as models, or as hypotheses that may be tested on the ground.

Given this most fundamental issue, a number of other limitations should be considered when modelling environmental factors using GIS, such as the question of resolution. What is the most appropriate resolution for any study of landscape? This may only be addressed by the response, what is the modelling intended to achieve? This question lies at the heart of all landscape archaeological studies and will depend on the nature of the questions being asked of the data. For example, addressing broad patterns of vegetation might be fine at a much lower resolution and over a much larger area than a study investigating the impact of vegetation on visibility patterns where the role of the individual is important.

Other issues regarding modelling limitations are more ephemeral, though arguably no less important. For example, how is it best to represent trees? Within three-dimensional representation packages, such as ESRI ArcScene, trees may be defined as individual objects but they may also be represented in bulk as polygons (e.g. Tschan 2000), and the decision between the two might be determined by the resolution of the study (*cf.* Higuchi 1983). It will also be dependent on the nature of the questions being asked. For example there becomes a real problem in modelling the visual impact of trees quantitatively by either method.

The last issue involves the role of GIS. If the modelling of environmental factors is likely to be incorrect on the basis of data extrapolation, then arguably the process is limited to visualisation. Whilst this visualisation is based upon collected data, interpolation levels are likely to be very high. At this juncture GIS may be considered as an analytical tool as well as a representational tool. In many ways the boundaries between graphics and analysis are becoming diminished.

THE IMPLICATIONS FOR OTHER STUDIES — LANDSCAPES AS HEURISTICS

Given the limits to modelling, what is the role of GIS within environmental modelling? The strength of any model lies in its ability to generate possible outcomes rather than realities. While it is not possible to know the exact location of every tree in the past (with the possible exception of submerged forests), this should not prevent us from trying. The advantage that GIS has is an ability to generate new data on the basis of older data. It is possible to begin to examine what a theory looks like in practice. A palynologist might mention that alder carr present in the pollen diagram is likely to occupy the low-lying valleys. Now it is possible to model where that is likely to be; to provide an illustration of a theory. Whilst the illustration might not be correct, it provides something 'on paper' that can be discussed and altered. As remarked by Gillings and Goodrick (1996), GIS really should increasingly be considered as a place to think, where the models being generated are thought of as heuristic models. In other words, perhaps the role of GIS in cases of such modelling is to provide scenarios from which it becomes possible to ask new questions and to learn from our own responses.

CONCLUSIONS

In normal circumstances it is impossible to predict the specifics of landscape change. Fundamentally, we cannot know exactly where individual trees were, or what their form might have been. However, GIS modelling of environmental factors enables us to consider what different types of data mean in the landscape context. Whilst the modelling is likely to have various levels of accuracy, even within a single model, it provides the opportunity to explore different pasts. This chapter has considered the modelling of vegetation from topographic data and from pollen data, and has addressed themes of physical landscape change and also shifts in sea level, and the impacts these changes might have had. Furthermore, it has considered some of the limitations of modelling approaches to archaeological landscapes. In the following chapter, the ways in which GIS may be used to address themes within theoretical approaches to landscape archaeology are addressed.

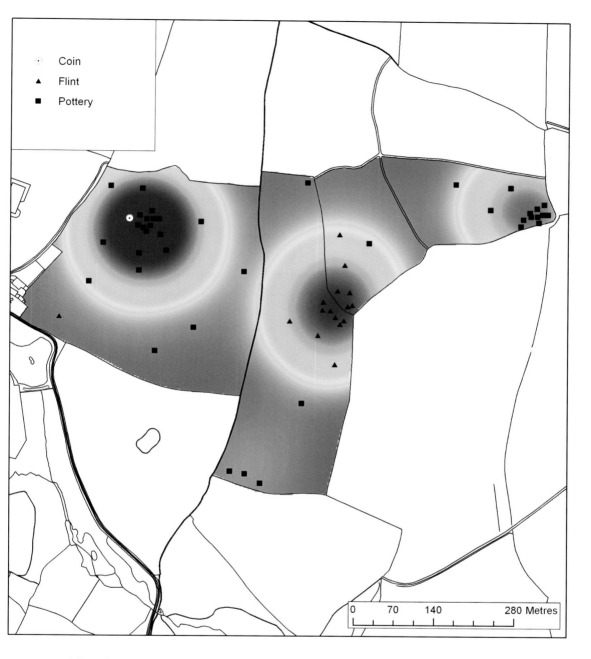

Coin

Flint

Pottery

0   70   140   280 Metres

1 Modelling find–density from fieldwalking data

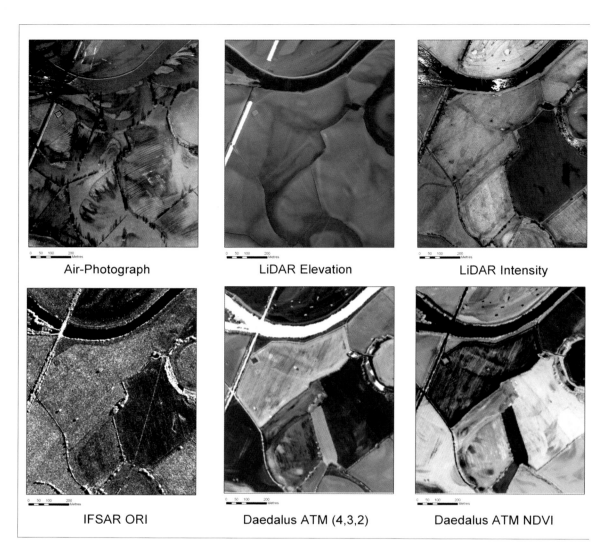

| Air-Photograph | LiDAR Elevation | LiDAR Intensity |
| IFSAR ORI | Daedalus ATM (4,3,2) | Daedalus ATM NDVI |

2 Comparing different types of remote sensing data from the confluence of the Rivers Trent and Soar in Nottinghamshire

3 Opposite above: Representing topography using grey shading for different heights

4 Opposite middle: The same area as *colour plate 3* represented by hillshading

5 Opposite below: Slope modelling identifying variations in gradient derived from the DEM shown in *colour plate 3*

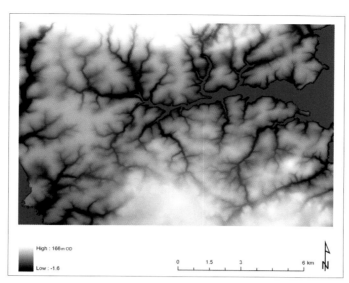

High : 166 m OD

Low : -1.6

0   1.5   3   6 km

N

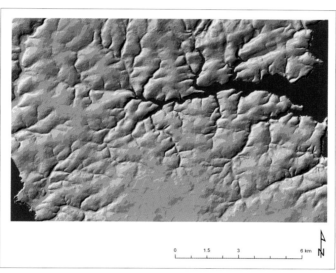

0   1.5   3   6 km

N

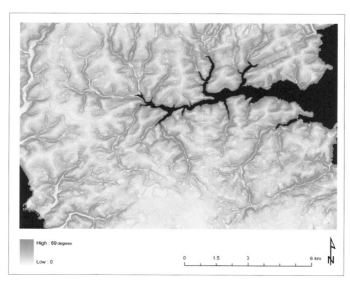

High : 69 degrees

Low : 0

0   1.5   3   6 km

N

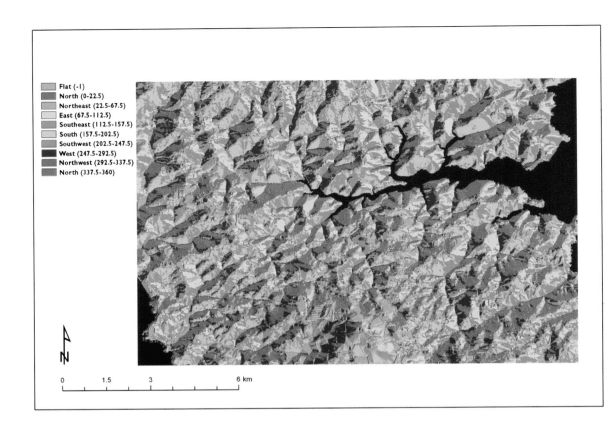

Flat (-1)
North (0-22.5)
Northeast (22.5-67.5)
East (67.5-112.5)
Southeast (112.5-157.5)
South (157.5-202.5)
Southwest (202.5-247.5)
West (247.5-292.5)
Northwest (292.5-337.5)
North (337.5-360)

N

| 0 | 1.5 | 3 | 6 km |

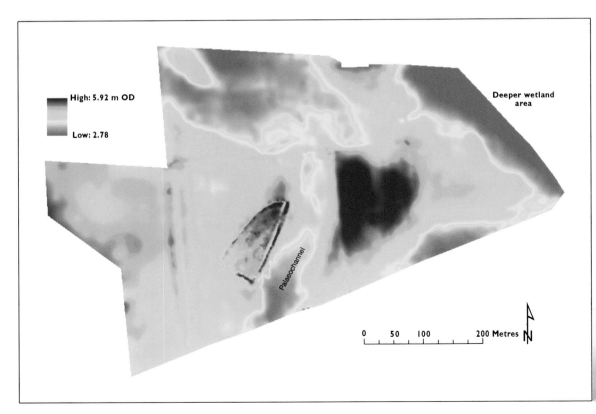

High: 5.92 m OD

Low: 2.78

Deeper wetland area

Palaeochannel

| 0 | 50 | 100 | 200 Metres |

N

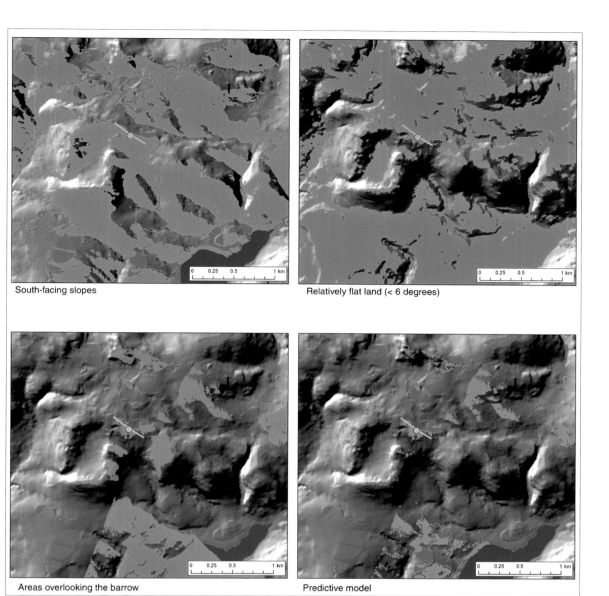

South-facing slopes	Relatively flat land (< 6 degrees)
Areas overlooking the barrow	Predictive model

8 Using predictive modelling to identify areas of likely Bronze Age agriculture based on the hypothetical rules of requiring south-facing slopes, relatively flat gradient and a view of an earlier barrow which remained in use during the middle Bronze Age at Carsington, Derbyshire (note that the reservoir would not have existed in this period)

6 Opposite above: Aspect modelling identifying which direction slopes face derived from the DEM shown in *colour plate 3*

7 Opposite below: DEM of the Sutton Common landscape showing 'islands' within the wetland, the palaeochannel and other local landscape features

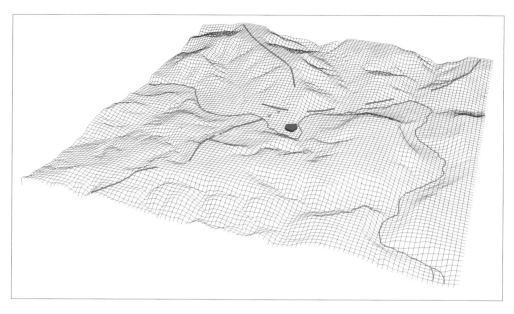

9 Using cost–path analysis to identify the likely position of a Roman road (in green) between known sections of the road (in red) surrounding Roman Bath (10 x 10km viewed from the south-east)

10 *Above:* Modelling geology along the River Rhine near Utrecht, Holland, to provide context for the positioning of Roman-period watchtowers. The model shows that routeways through the landscape were restricted to the dryland (in green) and the river itself since the alluvial wetlands (in cream) and peatlands (in brown) would have been less accessible. The watchtowers were therefore located to control movement along this narrow route (5 x 4km looking north-east)

11 *Opposite above:* Modelling of likely tree cover surrounding the Iron Age hillfort near Gear, Cornwall, based on slope, assuming that the steeper slopes would have been less easy to clear of vegetation (the hillfort enclosure measures 350 x 300m, viewed from the west)

12 *Opposite below:* Modelling sea-level change using multiple data sources to explain the Iron Age landscape of Green Island in Poole Harbour, Dorset. The two images show the present landscape and the reconstructed Iron Age landscape (16 x 16km viewed from the south)

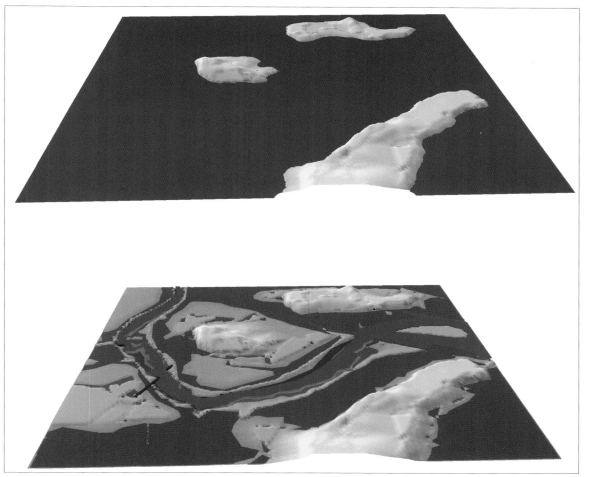

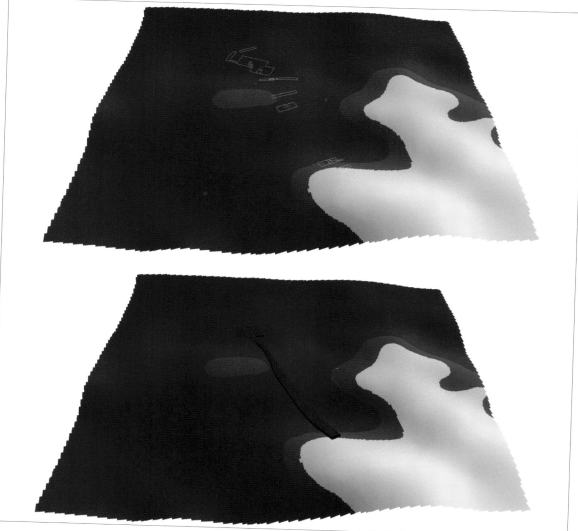

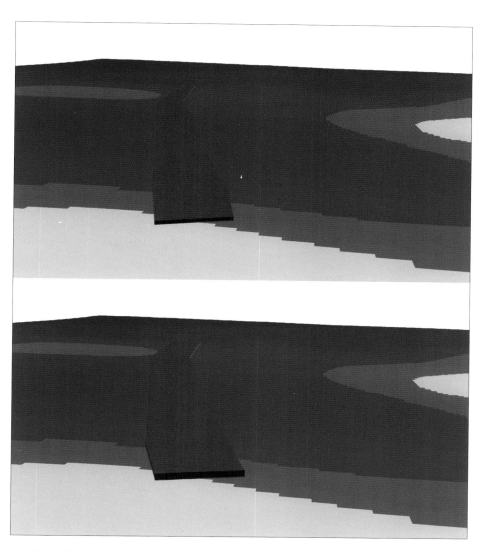

15 Above: View from the southern end of the later Neolithic trackway on Hatfield Moors. The first image shows the trackway as it is, narrowing along its length. The second image shows how different the site would have looked if it maintained a constant width. It seems likely that a factor in its architecture was to provide a more impressive view from this position in addition to controlling movement and access to the platform

13 Opposite above: Least-cost path from the shore to the Napoleonic Shorncliffe Redoubt based on slope. This route closely passes numerous defensive structures and thus would have been an unlikely approach for invaders. This is an extreme example of conceptual and cultural constraints to calculating cost of moving through a landscape

14 Opposite below: The local landscape context of the later Neolithic trackway and platform on Hatfield Moors, South Yorkshire. The first image shows the excavated features and the second image provides a simple reconstruction of the features (100 x 100m looking north)

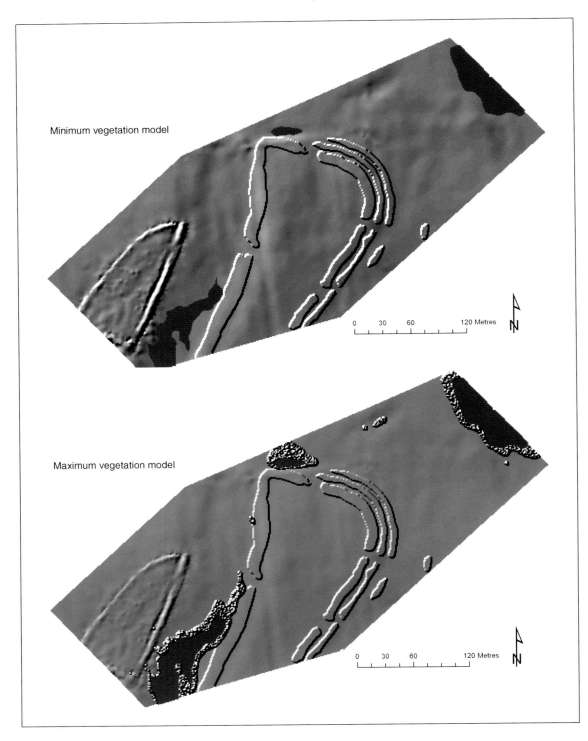

Minimum vegetation model

Maximum vegetation model

16 Maximum alder coverage and minimum alder coverage (cleared) models on Sutton Common, South Yorkshire

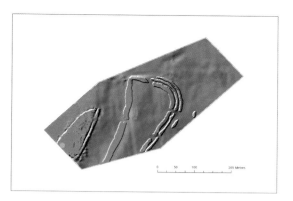
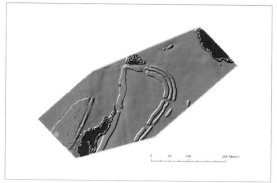
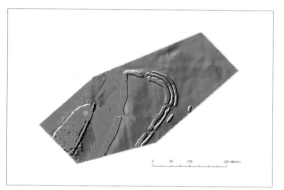
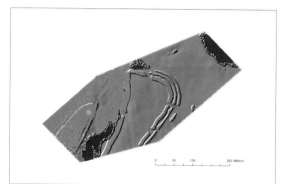
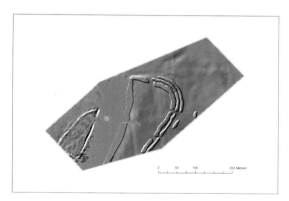
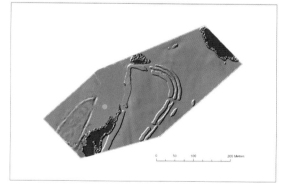
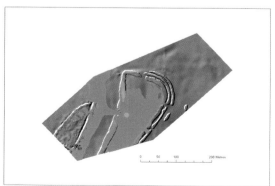
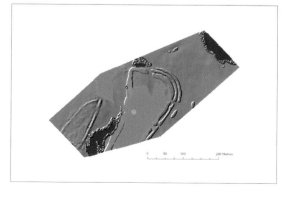

17 Comparing the visual impact of reconstructed vegetation at Sutton Common using viewshed analysis of both the minimum and maximum vegetation models

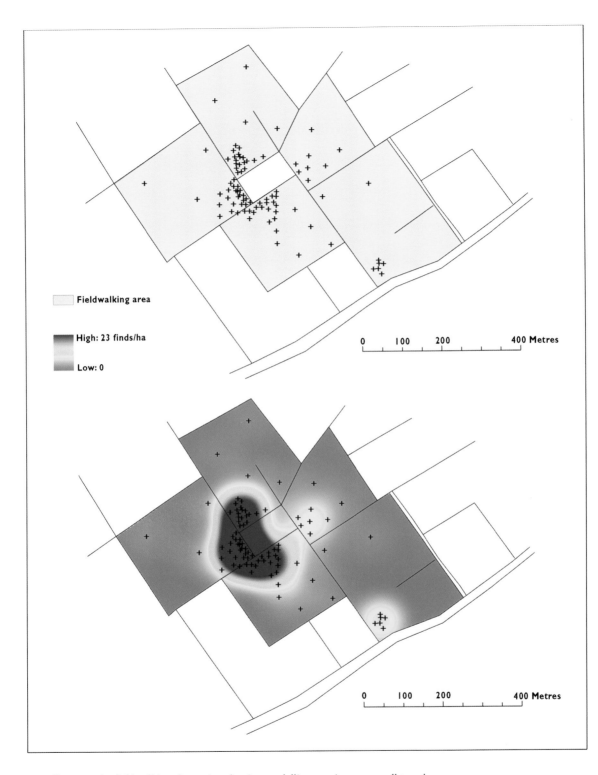

Fieldwalking area

High: 23 finds/ha

Low: 0

0   100   200   400 Metres

0   100   200   400 Metres

18 Filling gaps in fieldwalking data using density modelling to give an overall trend

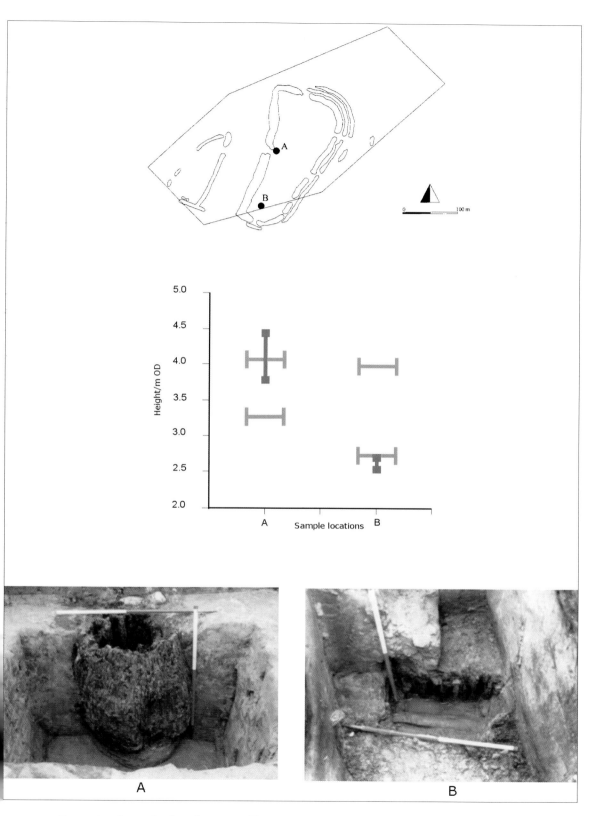

19 Comparing the results from the water table monitoring at Sutton Common with the preservation condition of excavated wooden remains

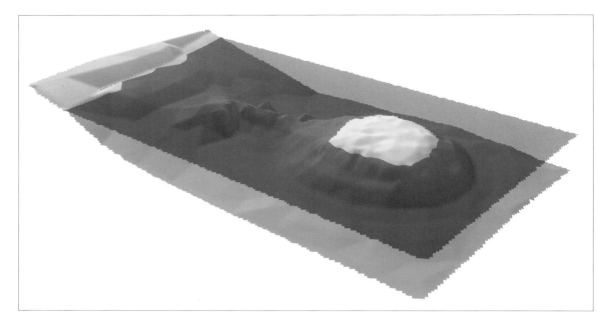

20 Crannog in Loch Migdale, Highlands. The site was underwater and surveyed using GPS from a boat. The resulting model shows the submerged landscape including the approach to the site from the loch edge (100 x 50m viewed from the south)

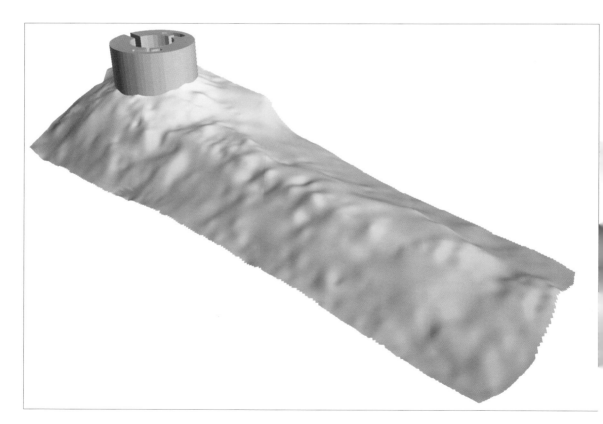

21 Applecross Broch, Highlands – ridge modelled from GPS data and overlain by an extruded polygon representing the structure based on excavated evidence to provide a simple visualisation (120 x 40m viewed from the north)

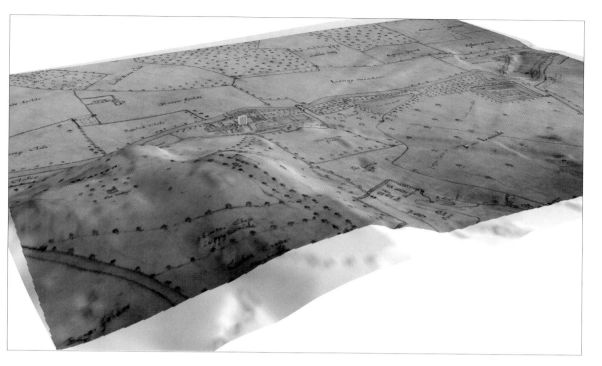

22 Integrating historical maps with topography – early seventeenth-century map of Esher, Surrey, with extruded buildings representing Wayneflete Tower (total area 1.3 x 1km viewed from the south-west)

23 Modelling vegetation based on a 1725 map of Chesham Bois, Hertfordshire. Combining topography, historical mapping, reconstructed trees and a reconstructed manor building (2.2 x 1.6km viewed from the east)

24 The Roman-period landscape of Dinnington, Somerset. The texture was derived from a variety of GIS analyses with the results being 'painted' in graphics software and draped over the DEM to provide a clearer visualisation of the landscape (4.5 x 3.8km viewed from the north-east)

25 Presenting results from GIS analysis using visualisation software – Northborough causewayed enclosure near Peterborough (overall diameter of the enclosure is 250m, viewed from the west)

8

Landscape archaeology and theory

INTRODUCTION

From a firmly epistemological perspective, it becomes increasingly difficult to place archaeological GIS within any single paradigm. Arguably, GIS software provides a positivist tool that can model various input data to provide quantitative results. However, GIS also provides a qualitative graphical interface. Blurring things further, GIS can provide a simulation of an environment at a given period through the stripping back of later features such as buildings and the reconstruction of environmental features. The simulation of past landscapes can enable them to be experienced in a virtual way. Such potential provided by GIS can feed into a number of theoretical themes used within landscape archaeology.

The central themes within landscape theory are underlain by the definition of landscape (*cf.* Olwig 1993). Tilley (1996) summarised the relationships between archaeology and landscape in four ways (also referred to in chapter 1):

1. as 'a set of relationships between named locales' (p. 161)
2. to be 'experienced and known through the movement of the human body in space and through time' (p. 162)
3. as 'a primary medium of socialisation' (p. 162)
4. creating 'self-identity' by controlling knowledge and thereby influencing power structures (p. 162)

From this the key principle may be considered to be that of experience, and thus studies of archaeological landscapes have been based upon an attempt to replicate the experience of 'Being-in-the-world' while trying to reconstruct the dialectic of the existential 'Being' (Tilley 1994, 12). To date, the primary method of measuring experience has been through the analysis of visibility patterns. For example, Thomas (1993) investigated the visual impact of monuments, particularly around Avebury, suggesting themes of inclusion and exclusion (similar to Tilley's fourth point, mentioned above). Devereux (1991) also analysed the spatial relationships between monuments and topography at Avebury by investigating their visual relationships. Similarly, Tilley (1994) investigated three archaeological landscapes through a photographic essay and by recording patterns of intervisibility between monuments.

With such dominance in the use of visibility patterns underlying so many theoretical approaches to landscape archaeological theory, GIS is well suited for exploring and presenting these theoretical approaches in a quantitative way. However, there are numerous other ways in which GIS may be used to address questions relating to theoretical approaches to landscape archaeology. As mentioned previously, GIS is becoming more of a 'place to think' (Gillings and Goodrick 1996) than merely a quantitative tool. This chapter explores some of the approaches that have been used to address these themes, in addition to suggesting a number of new ones.

SPACE AND PLACE

In his book, *Space and place – the perspectives of experience*, Tuan (1977) provided one of the bases from which experiential landscape archaeology has progressed (e.g. Tilley 1994). This work identified a dualistic approach to understanding our lived-in environment. 'Place is security, space is freedom' (Tuan 1977, 3). Put simplistically, landscapes consist of a series of places that are culturally constructed through the activities, stories or memories associated with them. The areas between places may be referred to as 'space'. This duality provides us with an opportunity to divide landscapes of different periods between places, perhaps occupied by buildings or monuments, and the spaces between them.

In terms of computing and GIS, the division of cultural landscapes into places and spaces, whilst overly simplistic in a prescriptive way, is extremely tangible and useful. On the ground, the definition of a significant 'place' at a given period may be explored by embodying that locale and experiencing the landscape, albeit in its modern form. Within the computer, this approach can again be used, but with the advantage of exploring different possible pasts, through the regression of the modern landscape, and the reconstruction of site distributions and perhaps environmental conditions.

A place that may be considered as an archaeologically significant position, perhaps due to the situation of a burial monument, can be examined for its visual impact, both from this place to its surrounding space, and inversely from the wider landscape to the particular site. What other monuments fall within the visible areas, which ones fall outside and which follow its horizon?

This technique has also been explored through digital landscape reconstruction. Fisher *et al.* (1997), for example, analysed the positioning of Bronze Age cairns, demonstrating a visual relationship between their positioning and corresponding view to/from the sea. In contrast, Lake *et al.* (1998) presented an approach to assess the hypothesis or observation that Mesolithic flint working sites were located in places that were significant due to the views they commanded, perhaps due to the potential for observing the movement of game. In order to test this, they created an automated approach which assessed the visibility from each cell within the study area DEM by calculating the number of visible cells within its viewshed. By automating this approach, they were able to obtain values for every cell within the model, which could then be compared with the number of visible cells from the Mesolithic sites. Hence, this enabled them to ask the question of whether the locations of flint working sites were more significantly superior in terms of viewshed than other possible areas within the landscape. Whilst considering the influencing factors, such as contemporary vegetation, the authors were able to quantitatively examine this hypothesis.

ROUTES OF MOVEMENT AND NARRATIVES OF VISIBILITY

In relation to archaeology, Tilley (1994) expanded the dualistic concept of space and place to include pathways where movement might occur between different places and through space. Using the example of the Dorset cursus, Tilley argued that different elements of the landscape as well as different monuments from earlier periods were experienced at different points along the route as part of the architectural design of the monument. Furthermore, he used this approach to argue that the cursus enabled movement along it in a particular direction and hinted at cursus function based upon this.

GIS provides the potential to explore these qualitative themes in a quantitative environment. Through the reconstruction of a landscape as a DEM, more recent features and trees, which on site would obscure the experience, can be eliminated. Furthermore, as discussed in the previous chapter, it is possible to reconstruct many of these elements of the landscape too. Hence the GIS provides the tool for experiencing the landscape of a given period without the clutter of features from later periods.

It is possible to examine the visual properties of monuments within a GIS, such as the Rudston cursus complex in East Yorkshire (Dymond 1966, Riley

1988, Stoertz 1997). Here, a group of four cursus (*cf.* Stoertz 1997) cluster around a bend in the Great Wold Valley on the Yorkshire Wolds (*41*). Two particularly interesting features may be considered in relation to this landscape. The first relates to the cluster itself, being the largest concentration of cursus monuments known, providing the possibility of comparing the results of one cursus study with another within the complex. Secondly, the shape of cursus A is unique insofar that it forms a dog-leg bend where cursuses are normally relatively straight (Loveday 1985, see chapter 6).

An examination of the routes of each of the cursuses, founded upon GIS-based visibility (Chapman 2005), revealed themes of interpretation and chronology (*42*). Of the cursuses only one stratigraphic link has previously been made; between cursus C and cursus D, showing D to be later. Stylistically, cursus A was considered to be the earliest of the complex (Loveday 1985). Using this loose framework, the visibility from positions at regular intervals along each of the cursuses was assessed in GIS. From this narratives were written for both directions of movement, for example north to south, and then south to north, linking back to the approach used by Tilley (1994, see above).

The results from this study identified that each of the cursuses appeared to display different priorities in relation to their architecture and visibility patterns. The potentially earliest cursus, cursus A, displayed a close visual link to long barrows on the western horizon which were maintained in that position throughout the route. This link to the earlier period also explained the dog-leg plan of the monument which appears to have been designed to maintain this visual pattern (Chapman 2003). This cursus also displayed themes of 'visual surprise' upon approaching the end of the monument, though this only worked when following in one direction of travel and not in the other. Tilley used such an observation to explain directionality of the Dorset cursus, and it appears that the same could be said for Rudston cursus A. cursuses B and C provided very similar visual responses to cursus A, but without the constant link to earlier monuments. Rather they maintained a link to cursus A, reinforcing the interpretation that this was the earliest of the group and thus emphasising Loveday's morphologically-based interpretation (1985). The key similarities were in the visual surprise elements at the end of the route, normally characterised by keeping the cursus terminus out of view until the very last few steps of the route whereupon it comes into view. Whilst the Rudston group have all been levelled by ploughing, visual surprise was demonstrated at the Dorset cursus by an enlarged, and thus more dramatic, terminus at this end. Rudston cursus D, in contrast, did not display any of the traits of the earlier cursuses, but rather formed an enclosure which linked the cursus group, and associated monuments at its southern end, with a visual link to a separate group of monuments to the north.

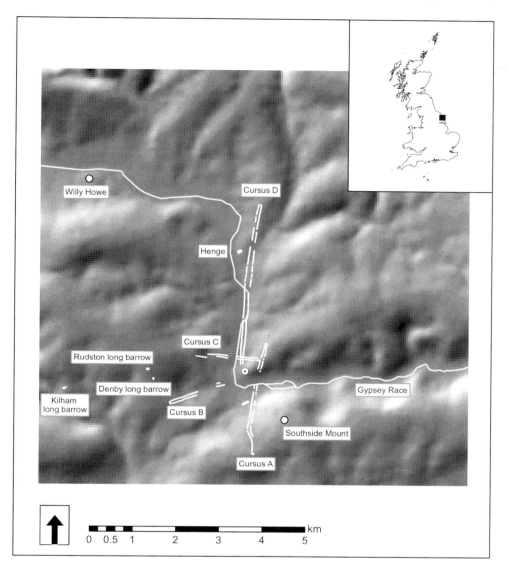

41 Location map of the later Neolithic monuments forming the Rudston complex on the Yorkshire Wolds, East Yorkshire

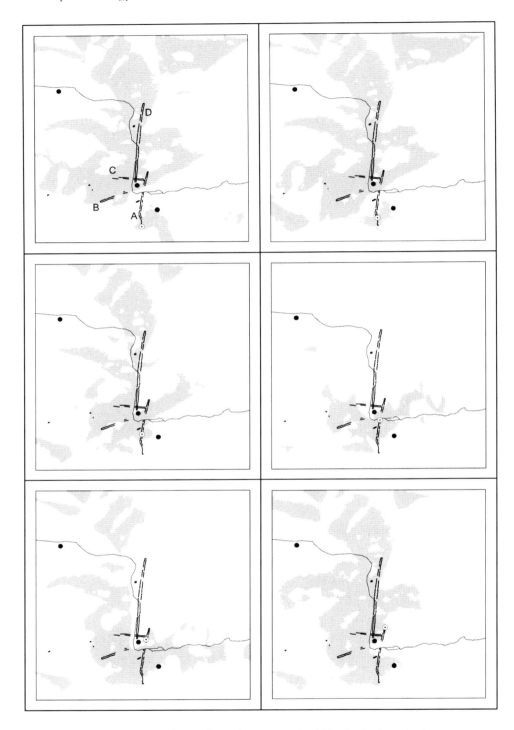

42 Changes in the viewshed when walking along cursus A within the Rudston landscape

The visual approach, following from Tilley's theoretical approach to interpreting the Dorset cursus, thus demonstrated apparently different functions between the monuments in addition to reinforcing the chronology of the landscape. The interpretations of function were also reinforced by the local landscape setting. The vast difference in visual response between cursuses A, B and C on the one hand and cursus D on the other was reflected by their relationships to the Gypsey Race stream running through the Great Wold Valley. Cursuses A, B and C all run perpendicular to the stream, with cursues A and C actually cutting across it, whereas cursus D is aligned with the stream and doesn't cross it (Chapman 2005). Hence it was possible to explore elements of essentially phenomenological approaches to landscape archaeology, albeit focusing on visibility, with confidence.

CUMULATIVE VIEWSHED ANALYSIS

A method used to address theoretical themes of landscape archaeology within GIS is cumulative viewshed analysis, first used by Wheatley (1995). The significance of a viewshed from a given point has been interpreted to suggest that the location of a site is significant due to the viewshed that it commands (e.g. Thomas 1993, Tilley 1994). Llobera (1996) applied these theoretical concepts to archaeological GIS studies, suggesting that GIS was not a limited, normative and reductionist tool, but rather had the potential to act as a heuristic tool; exploratory rather than dualistic. Multiple viewsheds were generated from the lines of the linear ditches on the Wessex chalklands to see if a similar area could be seen from either side. It was indicated by the analysis that the viewsheds were singly-directional, supporting the view that they were territory markers. A further level of cumulative viewshed analysis was then achieved through the creation of a *gradient view*. This used a cumulative viewshed formed by the combination of views of different distances (set at 50m intervals). For example, areas closer to the observer would be seen within each viewshed, whereas areas further away would be seen fewer times. The conclusions from this research suggested that the function of the linear ditches were to mark territories, but that these were not in the enclosed, inward-looking sense but rather as markers.

GIS has also been used as a tool to test hypotheses relating to visual significance of the type suggested by Thomas (1993) and Tilley (1994). The traditional (non-GIS) approach has been criticised by suggesting that the significance of a location based on visual factors can only qualified if it commands a significantly better view than other places within that landscape. In other words, a statement that a site was positioned in a certain location because it enabled a greater view of the surrounding landscape can only be considered accurate if a sample of other locations within that same landscape command inferior views (Fisher *et al.* 1997). The problem was addressed by comparing the view commanded by a series of cairns to the views from a series of 'non-sites' chosen randomly from the surrounding landscape. These were assessed in relation to views of the sea which had been previously interpreted to hold significance in relation to the siting of the cairns. The results from this work demonstrated that the hypothesis that there was a visual relationship between the siting of cairns and views of the sea was correct. Another study analysed Mesolithic site distribution, investigating the hypothesis that sites were located in positions that commanded better views by which to watch game (Lake *et al.* 1998). This study employed a GIS method which calculated the number of cells visible from each cell within the DEM, enabling comparison between cells occupied by sites and those without sites. The results demonstrated that the hypothesis was not robust.

MODELLING SIGNIFICANT PLACES UNOCCUPIED BY MONUMENTS

Bradley (2000) has demonstrated how natural places might obtain significance in a similar way to those areas normally ascribed 'place' through the identification of monuments or other archaeological features. Ethnographically, it is extremely common to have cultures ascribe significance to 'natural' places within a landscape which potentially might never deliver physical remains of cultural activity. In archaeology, the opportunity to identify significant places is rare. For example, a tree which might once have held significance will be long gone due to decay or felling. However, from the ethnographic record it is reasonable to assume that the positions of significant places might have had the same influence on the siting of new monuments as other earlier monuments might have had. To take the example of cursuses discussed earlier, the positions of early Neolithic long barrows appear to have had a significant affect on the architecture of later Neolithic cursus monuments (Chapman 2003).

Following this type of reasoning, Llobera (1996) demonstrated how GIS might be used to calculate the most likely positions of these 'significant places', with a view to investigating them on the ground. The technique he used was similar to the cumulative viewshed approaches commented on earlier (Wheatley 1995). At a simplistic level, it is possible to identify potential 'significant places' through the examination of monument placement for a particular period. For example, it might be appropriate to consider long barrow placement in the landscape (*43*). If an area was important at the time of barrow construction, then it is feasible that the barrows would have been constructed such that they each had a view of that

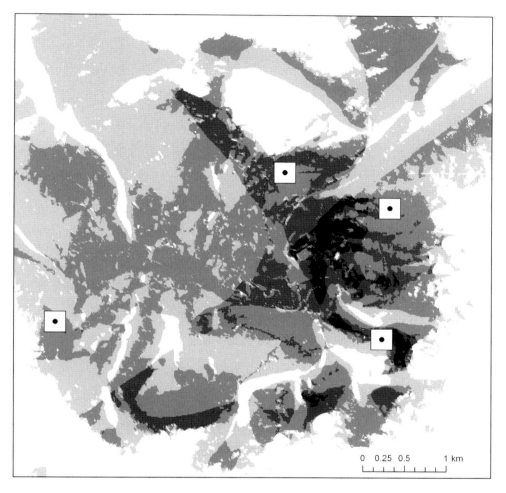

43 Using cumulative viewshed analysis to identify areas that overlap within the views from contemporary monuments. It may be argued that whilst such areas may be devoid of monuments, they may have been considered as culturally significant. *Cf Llobera 1996*

area, in addition to any other landscape placement themes. Taking this theory as the basis for a model, it is possible to assess this hypothesis by using cumulative viewshed analysis.

If each long barrow in the landscape is taken to be broadly contemporaneous, and the concept of significant place is seen as be appropriate, then it is possible to begin to model these places. By generating a viewshed model from each of the long barrows in the landscape, and then by adding these models together, areas of overlap may be identified. It is worth noting, particularly in the case of long barrows, that a lack of overlap has been used to interpret ideas of territoriality.

However, these overlaps between the viewsheds from each monument may also be considered to have been a significant place in the past (*cf.* Bradley 2000).

Whilst this provides just one example of how GIS can be used to hypothesise about potentially significant areas, it is possible to understand how such a technique may be used where evidence on the ground is not apparent. Equally the technique may be used for a number of different periods. Mesolithic tool production sites, for example, might have been focused around certain landscape features or significant places. Given the ease with which such analyses may be conducted, it seems appropriate that some level of predictive modelling of significant places from any dataset should be part of any prehistoric landscape project.

MODELLING CONCEPTUAL SPACE

It may be considered that, within human society, practical considerations are not the only ones which influence choice in terms of settlement, pathways through the landscape, or the building of monuments. Conceptual issues such as areas considered as 'good' or 'bad', perhaps in terms of physical or spiritual frameworks, will influence the position of cultural remains in a way that cannot be explained purely by environmental modelling. Even if a least-cost path demonstrates the 'easiest' route in terms of physical effort, it is possible that certain areas might have been avoided, leading to a bias in the results.

The problem of modelling conceptual space becomes very difficult in terms of GIS, although the issue can be addressed through heuristic modelling or hypothesis testing. In many ways, the model generates possibilities rather than realities. For example, it is possible to generate theoretic models using layers of interpretative data. The results from 'significant place' modelling might be used to either identify as a node of a route through the landscape, or as somewhere to be avoided. Similarly, it might be represented as a position where numerous viewsheds meet. Ultimately the nature of the archaeology will determine the types of conceptual model that are possible or appropriate, although it is worth considering how high levels of GIS-based modelling may be used to simulate conceptual landscapes (*colour plate 13*).

To take a basic example, it might be considered that boggy, wetland environments are culturally dangerous, following from ethnographic parallels. In a traditional functionalist model of movement, it might be appropriate to build cost–path models on the basis of how easy it is to physically traverse different types of landscape. The boggy area in question might be more difficult to pass through, say by a factor of 3. However, if we consider that the past cultural perception of that landscape was as a very dangerous area which should never be traversed, then the cost value of cells in the DEM relating to that landscape should be increased appropriately, perhaps to 10. Hence, any cost-path modelling through the landscape becomes culturally determined (theoretically) whereby the route chosen is a combination of ease of movement through the dryland landscape, coupled with a great level of avoidance of the wetland.

A further consideration when modelling cultural landscape is the role of the individual, so prevalent within phenomenological approaches. For example, the normal use of 1.7m for the height of an individual might be adapted if one is considering the role of children, women or the infirmed. Clearly, by altering the height of the observer, the potential for changing the results of visibility analysis becomes great, dependent upon the accuracy of the DEM. Furthermore, the role of disability in the past should not be ignored. Fundamentally, these aspects are rarely modelled, but provide an avenue towards exploring data in a multitude of ways.

There have been recent advances in developing GIS methods for addressing some of the issues of landscape perception. Llobera (2001) addressed the issue of landscape affordances; in other words, the specificities that the landscape offers a particular animal, which therefore applies directly to humans (Gibson 1986). Llobera's approach to this was to attempt to both define and model topographic prominence as significant places (*cf.* Tuan 1977). The prominence of a particular site was calculated as the percentage of locations (or cells) lying below an individual's position within a given radius. In this study, Llobera noted a demonstrable correlation between the locations of Bronze Age barrows and high levels of relative prominence. This was found to be in contrast with Iron Age square barrows within the Yorkshire Wolds study area which did not display the same levels of prominence. Thus it was argued that the positions of Bronze Age barrows were more likely to be related to areas that dominated the landscape, perhaps acting as territorial markers.

CONCLUSIONS

The realm of theoretical archaeology provides a number of methods for considering landscape archaeology. The most obvious of these is the use of phenomenological approaches, focusing on the role of the individual and their perception of the landscape. However, other themes may be incorporated, particularly through the adaptation of viewshed analyses, cumulative viewshed analyses, the construction of narratives of movement, and the use of 'cost' when generating cultural, as opposed to reconstructed 'natural', landscapes.

In this chapter, a number of different methods currently being used to address considerations of theoretical landscape archaeology have been explored. In principle, the key issues lie around the ability of GIS to generate repeatable quantitative models, with appropriate metadata, of landscape perceptions that are often not possible on the ground due to more recent building and landscaping work. The main point is that, whilst models may be generated, at the theoretical coalface these remain merely models. Whilst they might help to explain certain phenomena, these remain subjective and ultimately unknowable. In this framework, it appears that the most appropriate way of using GIS for theoretical landscape study is as a tool for exploring datasets, and the relationships between them, essentially using the software as a heuristic tool rather than an absolute one.

In terms of the future development of GIS, and of the spatial technologies more generally, it was noted over a decade ago that the growth of artificial intelligence systems and developed methods of simulation were likely to have a significant impact on archaeological theory in its broadest sense (Claxton 1995). Furthermore it was envisaged that, whilst GIS provided the central arena for collating different datasets, it would become recognised as a 'medium for theoretical discourse' (*Ibid.* 346). It seems that, over 10 years later, the development of GIS is becoming integral to much archaeological research, providing a foundation for this type of discourse.

<h1 style="text-align:center">9</h1>

<h1 style="text-align:center">GIS and landscape interpretation</h1>

INTRODUCTION

The previous chapters have considered landscape interpretation from the separate themes of positivist analysis, environmental reconstruction and landscape theory, exploring the ways in which GIS may be utilised to address aspects of each. However, in reality, landscape archaeology normally incorporates all three themes. Landscapes and sites within landscapes are considered in terms of (1) pragmatic themes of economics and practicalities, (2) how the physical and environmental landscape has changed, as well as (3) the different interpretations that alternative theoretical approaches may have.

In this chapter the themes from the previous three chapters are brought together using case studies to illustrate ways in which this might be achieved, although clearly the approaches and methods that can be used will be reliant on the type of archaeology, type of landscape and the availability of datasets. The advantage of GIS in this type of multi-faceted analysis is its ability to store, manipulate, analyse and visualise multiple datasets together.

ANALYSING THE NEOLITHIC LANDSCAPE CONTEXT OF A TRACKWAY AND PLATFORM

Raised mire peatland landscapes provide the potential for preserving organic archaeological remains due to high levels of saturation and the chemical conditions of the peat (Coles and Coles 1986). Within the raised mire of Hatfield Moors, South Yorkshire, the discovery and excavation of anthropogenically modified wooden remains have revealed a trackway and platform structure

44 Excavations of the later Neolithic corduroy trackway and platform on Hatfield Moors, South Yorkshire

45 The birch bark material which appears to form a 'threshold' between the trackway and platform of this later Neolithic site

extending from an area of dryland sand dune into the peat deposits (44). Its structure is largely complete, as both ends have been identified, and it extends over a distance of approximately 60m. Radiocarbon dating of the timbers has produced a later Neolithic date, between approximately 2900-2500 cal BC.

The structure consists of a corduroy trackway extending for about 50m before meeting the platform, the latter covering an area of approximately 10 x 5m. The structure of the trackway was formed by paired timbers, aligned with the direction of movement, overlain by unmodified transverse timbers forming the trackway surface. On its route the trackway also forms a slight dog-leg plan. The platform was of a similar surface construction, though with its timbers set obliquely to the trackway. However, the underlying structure was less systematic, with a combination of timbers and brushwood. At its landward end the trackway measured approximately 3m wide although, by its lower end to the north, it had narrowed to approximately 1m wide before meeting the platform. At its junction with the platform a band of white birch bark had been deposited on the surface, defining the difference between the two, indicative of a type of threshold (45).

The palaeoenvironmental evidence has indicated that the site was constructed during a period of increased local wetness, leading to something that may be tentatively described as a boggy pool. Furthermore, these deposits included the first instance of raised mire conditions which would have been dramatically different environmentally to any other landscape within the region, predating similar growth elsewhere on the mire by over 1000 years. Effectively, environmental change in this region would have resulted in a loss of dryland combined with the creation of an environmentally distinct area, quite different from anywhere else within the landscape, perhaps having its own intrinsic significance or importance to the local later Neolithic populations.

A number of research questions relating to the interpretation of the trackway and platform are clear from its architecture. Firstly, why does the trackway narrow before entering the platform structure? Secondly, why is there a slight dog-leg in the plan of the structure, given that the route would have been easy to create as a straight line if required over such a short distance? Thirdly, how does the trackway relate to the local topography and landfall effectively from dryland to wetland? Finally, what was the function of the trackway and platform during the later Neolithic? Previous research on trackways (e.g. Raftery 1996) has demonstrated three functions of trackways: to maintain routeways, to cross small areas of wetland or to access a part of the bog. Clearly it seems that the latter is appropriate for the trackway on Hatfield Moors, as it provides access to a platform situated within the contemporary wetland. In terms of platforms, sites are normally interpreted in relation to functionalist activites such as hunting or accessing a different set of resources (e.g. Ellis *et al.* 2002).

In terms of GIS-based interpretation, the first phase was defined by the digitising of the archaeological timbers to generate a spatial database of polygons representing each of the timbers, providing a plan of the site and a basis for further analyses. Secondly, a DEM of the sub-peat topography was generated by a grid of 111 boreholes, arranged over an area of 100 x 100m, set out at 10m intervals using differential GPS equipment. A stratigraphic survey undertaken at the same time accompanied the palaeoenvironmental record from the site.

The results from the subsurface topographic modelling in relation to the archaeological remains provided a DEM giving local context. The model revealed a spur of sandy dryland extending into the bog, though oddly the trackway was not positioned running into the peat from this perhaps obvious position, but rather from an area further back, indicating that the structure ran parallel to this spur. Clearly this suggested that, if the trackway was designed to access wetland environments (the third type of trackway mentioned above), then it was not in the most appropriate position, since an easier route into the wetland would have been possible from the end of the spur. Furthermore, the route of the trackway crossed a slight sub-peat ridge and area of higher land to the west before meeting the platform similarly identified by generating a profile of the route from the DEM.

The next phase was to integrate a representation of the palaeoenvironmental data within the model. From the excavation and stratigraphic survey, a layer could be generated in turn relating to the deposit of muds and to the 'pool' that was growing at the time the archaeological structure was constructed. This layer was added as a surface calculated in relation to the original sub-peat DEM, and draped over it. Hence, the resulting model displayed sub-peat topography with the DEM, with draped extents of the pool muds, showing areas of contemporary dryland and wetland during the later Neolithic period (*colour plate 14*). Over this was draped the polygon file representing the trackway and platform remains, including the birch bark deposit.

The composite model provided a basis for interpreting the site. Firstly, it provided a visualisation of how the topography, environment and archaeology related to one another. The initial observations of the topography in relation to the trackway were augmented through the consideration of the palaeoenvironmental layer. The model confirmed that what appeared to be a dryland spur was one, and that the trackway ran almost parallel to it. Furthermore, the trackway passed an area of relative dryland to the west, defined by a slight island which would certainly have been recognisable as drier than the surrounding muds – an area which would have been arguably more appropriate for the construction of the platform for accessing the bog's resources. It was also at this position that the first slight bend in the alignment of the trackway occurred, away from this topography, indicating that it was identified and was responded to during the later Neolithic. Similarly, the model demonstrated that, although the overall structure was approximately 60m long, the platform remained about 30m from the end of the spur. In practical terms it would have been much easier to construct a shorter platform from the spur than to create one nearly double the length.

From modelling the various layers and then considering the resulting model from various theoretical perspectives it becomes possible to construct a narrative of the site's function. The route of the trackway begins wide becoming narrow, enabling just single-file movement along it, thus determining the precise route that anyone accessing the platform would need to take, and perhaps framing the landscape before them. Arrival on the platform would have been marked by stepping over the 'threshold' defined physically by the band of birch bark. The large scale of the platform could have enabled a range of activities to have taken place, although archaeological evidence revealed sterility such that either no cultural remains were left, or that the site was purposely 'cleansed', perhaps in a similar manner to other later Neolithic monuments identified on dryland sites elsewhere (see Burl 1969). Anyone travelling along the trackway would have firstly experienced a fall in topography into the wetland. A slight rise would have been noticed as the very shallow 'island' would have been met by a small shift in direction away from this feature, although it would only have been noticeable as 'different'. The trackway would have been narrowing by this stage of the route, before bending slightly back, thus forming the dog–leg, just prior to stepping over the birch bark threshold and onto the platform. Throughout the route the procession could have been observed by spectators on the dry area to the east, defined by the sand dune. Even upon arrival on the platform, any activities could have been observed by any assembled audience within this area of dryland.

Considering the alternative theoretical perspectives in the interpretation of the archaeology, as defined by the composite GIS model, a number of conclusions can be drawn. Firstly, any positivist or processual interpretation of the site in relation to the practicalities of construction to achieve the ends of accessing the bog with a platform does not appear to fit the data. There are numerous other easier methods for accessing the bog, and arguably better areas to position the platform. The evidence of more effort, and subsequently more resources, than is required indicate that such a theoretical stance would be inappropriate. However, if the site is considered from a cultural geographic approach, the trackway may be considered as a processional routeway, positioned to enable different landscapes to be encountered as anyone passed along it, many to be seen at the same time; including dryland, relatively dryland, the pool muds and the infant raised mire. The narrowing of the trackway might reflect the importance of single–file access, perhaps as an architectural tool for ensuring that different features of the landscape are experienced in a prescribed manner (*colour plate 15*). The birch bark threshold provides a boundary from outside and inside the structure, thus emphasising the importance of arrival on the platform, as distinct from departure, in addition to reinforcing themes of exclusion and thus social differentiation. The platform can also be considered as something of a stage for ceremonial or other activities that could have been observed by 'excluded' people from within the community, whose presence would nevertheless have generated increased credibility for the 'performance' taking place on the platform. Within an interpretative framework such as this, all of the elements of data, including archaeological, topographical and palaeoenvironmental, begin to make sense. In this respect it may be more appropriate to consider the site as analogous to contemporary monuments such as henges, some of which have predetermined avenues or routes into the site, and where the architecture enables a sense of arrival within the site, coupled with a sense of inclusion for those involved in activities within the structure compared to the exclusion of those who aren't. It is possible that the banks of some henges may have provided a type of amphitheatre for spectators who were practically excluded by merit of features such as internal ditches, but who would lend integrity to the 'performance' within the henge as an audience. Indeed, there is evidence of henges being used as amphitheatres during the Roman period, such as Maumbury Rings,

46 Aerial photograph of Sutton Common, South Yorkshire, during excavation

Dorset. This may also be appropriate for sites such as Flag Fen near Peterborough which, although Bronze Age in date, consisted of complex trackway-like structures providing access to a large wooden platform where ceremonial activities such as the deposition of metalwork have been identified (Pryor 1991).

Without the use of the GIS to analyse the various layers of data for this site its interpretation is more likely to have been functionalist. However, the GIS-based modelling of these data has demonstrated that such an interpretation is unlikely to be correct. Rather, an interpretation of the site as relating to 'ritual', processional or ceremonial activities seems more appropriate, perhaps analogous to other contemporary sites such as henges, or later sites such as Flag Fen.

SUTTON COMMON — INTERPRETING AN IRON AGE LANDSCAPE

Sutton Common, mentioned briefly in chapters 6 and 7, is an area of former wetland in South Yorkshire. Here, a pair of enclosures occupies 'islands' on opposing sites of a relict infilled channel (*46*). The enclosures were previously defined by earthworks, although these were partially destroyed by bulldozing in the early 1980s (Riley 1982, Parker Pearson and Sydes 1997). The site was under arable cultivation for well over a decade, resulting in a relatively flattened and featureless landscape. The site was surveyed using GPS to generate data to create a DEM of the site. The resulting model was explored using hillshade and slope analyses to identify subtle features that could not be identified on the ground, including the positions of ditches due to the relative shrinkage of organic sediment within the ditches, causing a subtle dip in the surface topography. The survey also indicated that there might be a causeway linking the two enclosures (Chapman and Van de Noort 2001).

As part of the management of the landscape of Sutton Common, a number of analyses were undertaken between 1996 and 2003, including archaeological investigation, palaeoenvironmental study and assessment of the potential for *in situ* preservation (see chapter 10) which involved the GIS-based modelling of the groundwater table (Van de Noort *et al.* 2001, Chapman and Cheetham 2002).

The problems of interpretation of the enclosures on Sutton Common were based upon a number of architectural details that had been identified in the 1930s (Whiting 1936) and expanded upon in the 1990s (Parker Pearson and Sydes 1997). The earthworks of the two enclosures were very different. The smaller western enclosure was defined by a single bank and ditch, although the arrangement of these features was unusual. On its western side, the ditch was external in a traditional defensive form. However, its eastern side, adjacent to the relict palaeochannel, has an internal ditch, presumably much less defensible. The larger, eastern enclosure, in contrast, was defined by a single bank along its western edge, but with a double bank on its northern and eastern sides, and a triple bank around its north-eastern corner. Furthermore, early excavations of the site had revealed that the western side of the larger enclosure had been constructed using a white, limestone revetment, with stone brought from off site. Despite the unusual nature of these earthworks there seemed no clear way of explaining them. However, it was suggested that due to the proximity of appropriate drylands to the west it seemed likely that the site would have been approached from that side and that the smaller enclosure may have acted as a type of annex to the larger, eastern enclosure (47). Furthermore, this interpretation was strengthened by the presence of the white limestone wall that would have been markedly visible on approach (Parker Pearson and Sydes 1997).

The interpretation of the site was addressed through the use of GIS. The landscape model provided the basic layer for analyses, with the positions of the bulldozed earthworks reconstructed from the 1930s plan of the site (Whiting 1936, *cf.* Chapman 2001) and the ditches cut to their original depths following previous excavation evidence (Parker Pearson and Sydes 1997). These models were generated by creating a flat surface with cell values of 0 at the same

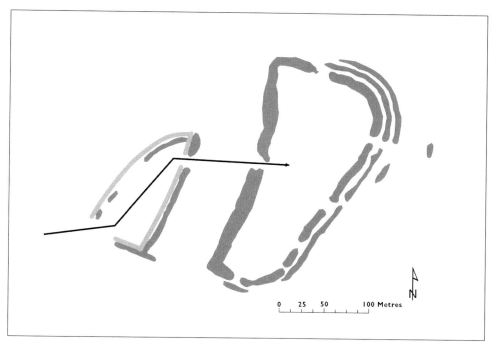

47 Outline plan of the Sutton Common enclosures showing route through the site, highlighting the unusual arrangement of ditches forming part of the smaller enclosure. *After Parker Pearson and Sydes 1997*

resolution as the DEM. Polygons representing the banks and ditches were converted to rasters, such that the ditches were given appropriate negative values and the banks appropriate positive values. The resulting raster was then added to the DEM, the resulting model being a composite of each of these layers.

The next step was to reconstruct the Iron Age water table to explore areas of groundwater. By averaging the multiple groundwater models, based on monthly measurements of 50 monitoring points over two years (Van de Noort *et al.* 2001, Chapman and Cheetham 2002), it was possible to get a shape of the water table, doming under the islands occupied by the enclosures. This was then raised to a level appropriate with the contemporary preserved organic deposits identified through palaeoenvironmental analyses. The resulting reconstructed water table model could then be subtracted from the DEM to examine areas of standing water and the depth of water both above and below ground. By subtracting the water table model from the DEM negative values in the resulting model represented standing water, whereas positive values reflected water below ground surface. Draping the resulting model over the DEM, highlighting areas of standing water, made the first step towards the interpretation of the earthworks.

There was a direct correlation between areas of the larger enclosure displaying fewer earthworks and those areas adjacent to the enclosure where there were expanses of surface water. This was thus interpreted as reflecting architectural choice, whereby the surface water could be considered as a part of the 'defences', replacing the need for banks and ditches in these areas, but reinforced by multi-valeting where no water was present (Chapman 2001).

The palynological record from the site had identified large quantities of alder (*Alnus*) within the close vicinity of the site during the Iron Age. The question of whether alder was growing in the palaeochannel provided a different way of considering the white limestone walling of the western side of the larger enclosure. Alder vegetation would have potentially obscured the view of the white limestone as the site was approached, contrary to the opinion that this was constructed in order to make the site look more impressive on approach. The visual impact of the potential vegetation on the site was addressed using GIS. As mentioned in chapter 7, alder vegetation is known to thrive within wet conditions, but not to enjoy extremely wet conditions. Using the modelled water table depths below and above ground surface it was possible to bracket the ideal growing conditions for alder trees to thrive on the basis of water alone. This area of the model was extracted using a raster calculator and used to generate a model of maximum alder vegetation on site. Alder was created using a random function for the height of cells between 0-8m, reflecting the range of heights of alder trees, with the resulting model being added to the DEM. An additional model was created with the alder vegetation 'trimmed' in areas of archaeology such as within the enclosure, within the ditches or upon the causeway between the two enclosures.

The results of these analyses were manifest as three principal models (*48*). Firstly, there was the basic DEM of the site with the reconstructed earthworks. Secondly, there was the former DEM but with reconstructed maximum potential spread of alder vegetation. Thirdly, there was the model of the water table, displaying different depths of water across the site. By draping the water table model over each of the other two models it was possible to create two scenarios (*colour plate 16*). The first showed the reconstructed landscape with surface water, but assuming that all of the local alder vegetation had been cleared, referred to as the 'minimum vegetation model'. The second, the 'maximum vegetation model' consisted of the reconstructed maximum possible extent of alder vegetation integrated with the DEM, with areas of standing water between tree clumps also shown; such areas of standing water were considered too deep for alder to grow successfully.

48 Opposite: Combining different models from Sutton Common, South Yorkshire – reconstructed earthworks, earthworks with reconstructed trees and areas of likely stranding water and surface wetness during the Iron Age

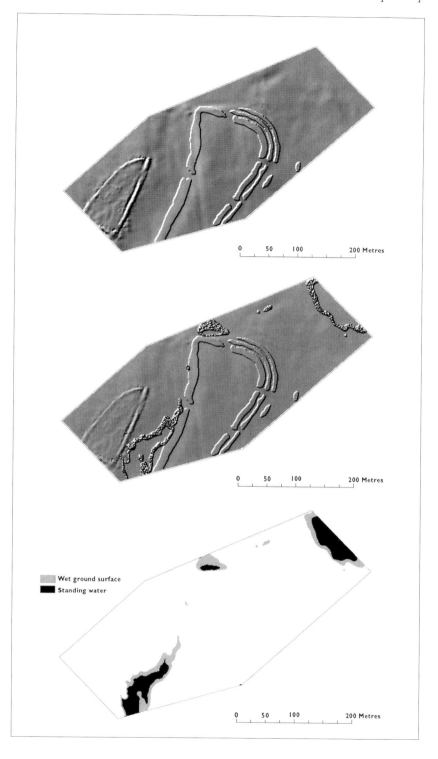

A theoretical approach was used to analyse the two models following established methods of constructing narratives based upon commenting on what is visible whilst moving through the landscape and, particularly, how this pattern changed (*cf.* Tilley 1994). The pathway constructed through the site followed that interpreted by Parker Pearson and Sydes (1997), entering the smaller enclosure from the west, exiting through its eastern break in the earthworks, crossing the palaeochannel causeway and entering the larger enclosure through its western entrance. Each model was interpreted in turn, with narratives constructed from the shifting visibility models (Chapman 2000, Gearey and Chapman 2005) (*colour plate 17*).

At the start of the route through the 'minimum vegetation model' (Chapman 2001), most of the earthworks of the enclosures were visible, including the position of the white limestone wall. Following the route through the smaller enclosure, the internal ditch of its eastern side began to make sense as a second line of defence, indicating that the earthworks represented something more akin to outworks than an enclosure. Upon exiting the smaller enclosure and walking across the platform, the view of the archaeological earthworks and the general surrounding landscape became increasingly restricted, whereby only the very local environment was visible. This may be interpreted as an architectural detail prompting increased feelings of anticipation in the person moving through the landscape. In contrast, upon arrival the view was nearly complete within the enclosure, but very rarely extended outside it, despite the reconstruction of the banks being only very slight so as to avoid their being deterministic in viewshed analysis. This may be seen as reflecting a sense of arrival within the site, whereby the uncertainty of 'outside' or the wildscape (*cf.* Ingold 2000) is diminished.

The analysis of the 'maximum vegetation model' provided surprisingly similar results, despite the masking effect of the trees (Gearey and Chapman 2005). On the approach to the smaller enclosure from the west, most of the site could be seen, although the earthworks defining the eastern side of the larger enclosure were more visible than those on the western side due to the masking by the trees. Upon leaving the eastern side of the smaller enclosure, and upon traversing the causeway across the relict channel, the diminishing viewshed was again noted, although in this case even more so due to the trees, with only small sections of the white limestone wall visible through the vegetation. Upon arrival within the larger enclosure again only the interior was visible, although the difference between the domestic 'inside' and the wild 'outside' was exaggerated due to the visibility of the trees surrounding the enclosure. Thus the trees could be interpreted as being potentially integral to the cognitive impressions intended by the architecture, emphasising the psychological effect of entering the site.

CONCLUSIONS – HOLISTIC LANDSCAPE INTERPRETATION

The integration of different approaches to landscape interpretation is made possible within GIS due to the capability to visualise and analyse multiple layers of data, both collected and hypothetically modelled. On different sites the availability of data will vary and so some approaches will be possible while others won't, except using hypothetical data. Even then, however, the value of GIS to provide metadata means that interpretations can be backed up by repeatable processes that can be altered at a later stage.

The case studies in this chapter have demonstrated how the integration of multiple datasets within the GIS can dramatically alter an interpretation based upon the traditional results from archaeological research or fieldwork. Each layer of data can be adjusted or remodelled using newer data, and so the GIS really does become a 'place to think' and to explore and visualise the data.

10

Cultural resource management

INTRODUCTION

Until now, the emphasis of this book has been placed on landscape archaeology from the perspective of interpretation. This interpretation has been addressed through landscape analysis, environmental reconstruction and landscape theory. However, commonly the role of the landscape archaeologist is to address issues of management, and particularly the management of the cultural resource. It can be the principal role of many GIS analysts to investigate the likely impact of a development, for example. This chapter, therefore, considers some of the ways in which GIS may be used to assist with the problems of cultural resource management, including the consideration of correlating layers of spatial data, predicting where archaeology might be in unsurveyed areas.

COMPARING LAYERS OF DATA

One of the most common uses for GIS in archaeology is as a data management tool. This is frequently used in record offices such as Sites and Monuments Records (SMRs) where sites may be represented as dots on maps, which can be interrogated if, for example, a new development is being proposed in their vicinity, thus supporting the decision process relating to mitigation. These types of GIS are becoming increasingly sophisticated, although different record offices address the technology in different ways. The potential to assess multiple layers together holds the potential for providing an extremely effective management tool (Gillings and Wise 1998).

A database aimed at development mitigation may have multiple layers of data that, hypothetically, could include: (1) a point file representing archaeological sites, find spots and so forth, including information relating to how and when it was found, where to find more information, and what the find represents. Essentially, such a database can be as complicated or as straightforward as desired, (2) a modern map layer at an appropriate scale, commonly using 1:10,000 scale raster layers, but could be represented as vector maps against which the positions of archaeological sites finds and any potential development may be compared, (3) historical maps, normally as raster layers, (4) polygon files relating to areas such as SSSIs (Sites of Special Scientific Interest) or those covered by legislative archaeological protection, (5) geological mapping, either as vector or as raster files, and (6) aerial photographic interpretation, again either as vector or raster files, such as the results from the various National Mapping Programmes conducted regionally by English Heritage (e.g. Stoertz 1997, Bewley 1998).

Additional data sources have been added to the normal range through particular regional and national studies in the UK. For example, a GIS-based initiative was undertaken to provide SMRs with a spatial layer relating to the potential for finding wet-preserved archaeological sites and deposits based upon an interpretation of known sites and the local geological conditions (Van de Noort and Powelsland 2001).

Online web-based GIS databases of interest are also available, some of which are directly archaeological, whilst others are of conceptual interest. A number of regional record offices currently offer their data (normally set to lower accuracy location information for sites and finds) freely over the internet. Similarly, the Archaeology Data Service (ADS), a part of the Arts and Humanities Data Service (AHDS), offer a range of spatial databases over the internet relating to archaeological projects, sites and finds throughout the UK (http://ads. ahds.ac.uk). Another, though non-archaeological, GIS-based internet service is provided by MAGIC, the Multi-Agency Geographic Information for the Countryside (www.magic.gov.uk).

Whilst these datasets provide useful information for research, arguably their primary aim is towards Cultural Resource Management, particularly through the use of known sites (as in the SMR or HER) or the potential for future sites (e.g. Van de Noort and Powelsland 2001) as a basis for managing mitigation of changes in land use or development works.

INVESTIGATING GAPS IN THE DATA

One of the principal problems in cultural resource management is that we are dealing with an unknown resource. Arguably, the locations of known sites and finds are more likely to reflect the distribution of previous archaeological work than the real distribution of the archaeology itself. It is often difficult to know whether a gap in distribution is a factor relating to the lack of occupation during a certain period, or a lack of systematic archaeological investigation. In research, archaeologists are more likely to keep visiting areas of known archaeology, and in terms of mitigation, the potential damage of a new development is more likely to be highlighted if there are known sites from the area as opposed to blank areas (*colour plate 18*).

One of the values of GIS is its ability to create new data layers from other datasets. For example, in terms of site distribution, if sites are not known from an area due to a lack of previous fieldwork, it is theoretically possible to generate rules from a similar landscape which has revealed archaeological sites and to apply these rules to the new landscape. By doing this it becomes possible to begin predicting where potential sites might be found on the basis of the rules that are applied to the GIS modelling, which assists in their management.

PREDICTING THE IMPACT OF DEVELOPMENT ON A LANDSCAPE

There has been a large corpus of GIS work aimed at predicting the locations of sites, typically within landscapes where there has been little archaeological investigation on the ground. In such cases the locations and densities of sites is unknown. When a development threatens the landscape it becomes important to be able to make management decisions on the basis of the potential for archaeological sites. GIS has been used to address this problem, particularly within north-western Europe and the USA. For example, forestry in an area is likely to damage any archaeological sites that might be present, but the size of areas used for forestry might be too large to effectively survey on the ground. In these cases, predictive models may be constructed in order to establish where best to direct archaeological fieldwork.

Predictive modelling of archaeological site locations is commonly approached through the identification of patterns within areas of known archaeology in relation to landscape factors. Such factors might include elevation, distance to resources such as water, aspect and slope gradient. For example, it might be noted that prehistoric field systems within a particular area are normally on south-facing slopes with a very slight gradient, perhaps maximising climatic conditions and preventing flooding. These factors can be identified and quantified within the GIS through surface analyses. Using the same analyses it is possible to examine a much larger landscape to highlight all other areas that display those same landscape properties as a method for directing fieldwork.

The use of GIS for the predictive modelling of archaeological site locations as part of cultural resource management has been criticised on the basis that any model can only be as good as the data from which it is created and the rules that are generated subjectively about site location. Ultimately, it can only be fortuitous if a GIS predictive model accurately identifies the location of a particular site. This issue has been addressed in a number of ways, including the generation of models based on only a proportion of the total archaeological dataset, so that the accuracy results can be quantitatively understood in relation to whether it found the remaining sites in the database.

The nature of predictive modelling using GIS is a subject that may be as complex or as basic as seems required. Many approaches use relatively complex statistics to analyse site distributions and the likelihood of finding new sites (Westcott and Brandon 2000). An approach aimed at getting over the issue of accurate prediction of sites specifically was provided by Warren (1990a, 1990b). Rather than attempt to predict site locations, he addressed the problem firmly from the cultural resource management arena, and particularly that of mitigation. Warren's approach was to identify areas rather than sites of greater likelihood of finding sites, using what he called a 'Red Flag Model'. Essentially, the approach was aimed at highlighting regions that would be likely to cost more money in terms of archaeological mitigation than others, based on the likelihood of finding sites. This way, rather than attempt to locate archaeological sites, he was identifying hot spots for developers to avoid.

In some cases, the nature of the predictive approach becomes more particular. In some landscapes, environmental change might mean that the modelling becomes more complex with the need for additional layers of data. For example, in floodplains much archaeology might be concealed beneath layers of alluvium or in peat bogs, the growth of peat will mask archaeological sites. In these cases predictive models may be based upon the generation of models of environmental change by which to address where different types of monument are more or less likely to exist (Chapman and Gearey 2003). Whilst this type of approach clearly strays into the environmental determinism debate, the approach offers the capability to provide cultural resource managers with a kind of 'red flag model' of where sites of different periods are more likely to be discovered and thus where some consideration of mitigation for developers should be undertaken. In the case of raised mires or peatlands, the vertical growth of organic matter will preserve organic remains. Because the peat is datable, it becomes immediately possible to provide *a terminus post/ante quem* for potential archaeology that may be contained within a section. If the lateral growth of peat can also be dated accurately and modelled within the GIS, it also becomes possible to identify where the edge of the bog is at a given date. This bog edge is likely to be the most intensively occupied or used part in the past due to the variety of resources available within the conjoining landscapes and the area where structures could be built even when the bog was inaccessible. By adding other palaeoenvironmental data it becomes possible to develop such a model in terms of accessibility to the surface of the bog at different periods. Palaeovegetation will provide some clues to this, as will the results from analyses such as of testate amoebae, organisms which provide information on the relative water table levels at different times, and the levels of surface dryness (Charman and Chambers 2004). Clearly at drier times the surface of the bog would have been more accessible compared with wetter times, and thus the distribution of archaeological sites might be spatially wider. Such analyses can be extremely complex with multiple datasets being represented and visualised. However, by integrating data relating to the palaeoenvironment, the potential distribution of sites from different periods becomes more feasible.

The difficulties attached to predictive modelling are the same as for any other type of modelling. Primarily, the output is only as good as the data upon which the generalisations are made. There is consequently a tendency to be accused of environmental determinism (e.g. Gaffney and van Leusen 1995), even though normally a combination of environmental factors (such as topography) are commonly used in conjunction with archaeological distributions. Clearly not all human activities are determined by environmental conditions, such as climate and topography, although the conditions provide the arena for human activity. Given the range of GIS-approaches that may be used in the interpretation of archaeological sites (e.g. chapter 9) perhaps a similarly integrated approach may be appropriate for predicting the locations of archaeological sites for cultural resource management.

A further criticism of the predictive modelling of archaeological site location using GIS is based upon the results. If a predictive model is tested and appears to work, then there is the possibility of circularity. In other words, if sites are predicted, then there is the potential that the GIS model will be considered correct. Even if it is refined with additional discoveries, there is the chance that its results will become a self-fulfilling prophesy, with the potential of missing additional sites that fall outside of its parameters.

ASSESSING CHANGE

A further aspect of cultural resource management is monitoring change to a site or landscape that might be detrimental to its *in situ* preservation. The problem is that rate of change cannot always be appreciated, nor can its impact on the heritage resource. One of the most complex examples of change affecting archaeological site or landscape preservation is the de-watering of wetland sites, where damage is below the ground and thus invisible (see below).

49 Erosion of the Humber foreshore between Melton and North Ferriby

The most obvious example of assessing change in archaeological sites is through erosion (*49*). This might be the physical erosion of the archaeology itself, although this is often identifiable visually on the ground with little requirement for GIS-based approaches.

Where GIS becomes more useful is where an unknown resource is being eroded or damaged, such as through coastal erosion. To use a case study, the Humber Estuary has produced some of the most important sites relating to prehistoric seafaring activities internationally. The discovery of the Ferriby boats (or perhaps more appropriately called ships) on the northern foreshore between the 1930s and 1980s (Wright and Wright 1939, 1947, Wright 1990, Wright and Churchill 1965, Wright *et al.* 1989, Wright and Switsur 1993) have more recently been dated (Wright *et al.* 2001), revealing them to be the oldest seagoing vessels outside Egypt. In addition to the remains of at least five vessels, other structures have been discovered in the vicinity including the remains of two middle Bronze Age trackways within the area of Melton, highlighting the international importance of this area of foreshore (Fletcher *et al.* 1999). However, the peat and alluvium deposits that preserved these structures is being actively eroded by the shifting channels in the estuary.

A two-dimensional GIS-based approach was used to address the rate of erosion along this stretch of foreshore, and to investigate whether certain areas of this stretch were being eroded any faster or slower than others, providing information that may enable its management (Chapman *et al.* 2001). Data were captured using differential GPS of the edge of the peat shelf in two areas.

The first, at North Ferriby, covered a total length of 610m of the foreshore, and at the second, near Melton, a stretch of 140m was investigated. The peat/alluvium shelf was surveyed using GPS in 1997 and 2000. Additional layers of data were provided from vertical aerial photography, with each photograph scanned and georeferenced before digitising the position of the peat shelf. For North Ferriby, an additional layer of information was provided from the site plan during the excavations published in 1989 (Wright *et al.* 1989), although this data proved to be inaccurate and was omitted. At Melton, however, excavation plans from the 1980s proved to be more useful. Thus at North Ferriby, data were available for 1947 (aerial photography), 1997 and 2000 (differential GPS survey), whereas at Melton data were available for 1947 (aerial photography), 1987 (archaeological survey), 1997 and 2000 (differential GPS survey).

The results of the analysis enabled the quantification of the resource, and made it possible to begin to predict rates of erosion of each area of the peat/alluvium shelf, and the implications for any archaeological features contained within these deposits (*50*).

At Melton it was shown that, over the 140m stretch, a total of 12.4m had eroded over the 53 years represented by the data sources, or 0.23m per year

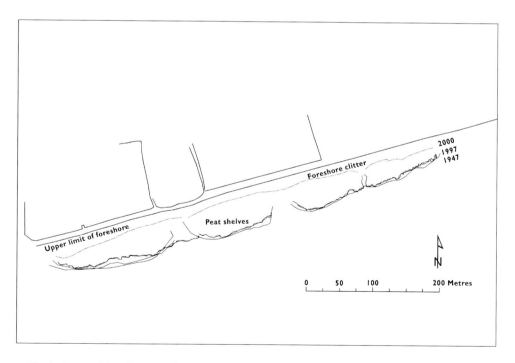

50 Exploring spatial and temporal erosion rates of the Humber foreshore at North Ferriby

on average. However, by comparing the datasets, it was shown that the rate of erosion had increased over time, from 0.12m/year between 1947 and 1987, to 0.56m/year between 1987 and 1997, to 0.73m/year between 1997 and 2000. This indicated that, of the 53 years studied, 17.6 per cent of the total erosion had occurred during the last three years of the study. At North Ferriby the area of foreshore was broken down into four roughly equally sized areas located around the positions of outfall pipes. Between the different areas the rates of erosion varied greatly, although in each case, erosion had accelerated more recently. Between 1947 and 1997, area 1 was eroding at a mean rate of 0.14m/year, increasing to 0.27m/year between 1997 and 2000. Area 2 increased from 0.07m/ year to 0.33m/year; area 3 increased from 0.04m/year to 0.17m/year, and area 4 increased from 0.05m/year to 0.57m/year. This showed that, whilst the erosion in each area appeared to be increasing, area 4's increase had been the most dramatic and area 3 had been least dramatic.

Overall, this analysis demonstrated how, within these two areas of the Humber Estuary, erosion had markedly increased over time, but also that rates of erosion were extremely localised, indicating that global estimates of erosion on the foreshore more generally were mainly useless when considering the impact on the archaeological resource of these landscapes. This conclusion reflects that of other studies in erosion which make a distinction between 'lumped' erosion models and distributed models, the latter taking into consideration the spatial component of processes (Verhagen 1996). In terms of GIS methods, this approach was two-dimensional, not taking into account the volumetric issues which have resonance for archaeological deposits contained within the peat/alluvium shelf. This would have been possible to model using borehole data from across the site by interpolating it into a raster dataset rather than as a series of vector lines as was used in this study. By three-dimensional modelling of the deposit it would have been possible to have modelled volumetric loss, and to provide a clearer understanding of the potential for archaeological deposits. Furthermore, it would have been possible to quantify surface erosion rather than just the erosion of the edge of the shelf.

WETLANDS

The use of GIS for cultural resource management can extend beyond the assessment of current data sources into a more active role. In the case of wetlands a number of particular approaches may be used in addition to the earlier factors. Wetlands provide increased potential for the survival of organic materials such as wood or leather, which themselves provide an increased level of data from which to understand the past. In terms of their management however they are arguably under a greater range of threats than most archaeological landscapes. In addition to the normal threats to archaeological sites such as development or physical damage, wetlands, and particularly the wet archaeological resource, may be damaged through drainage and water abstraction at the landscape scale. Extracting water from the soil means that archaeological sediments dry out and organic deposits may desiccate.

In recent years there has been an increase in interest in the management of wet archaeological sites and landscapes. However, traditional methods of excavation have been noted to actively damage the deposits that they are supposedly assessing. Consequently, there has been a move towards monitoring and modelling environmental conditions in relation to the archaeological layers.

The site of Sutton Common, South Yorkshire, has been discussed previously in relation to landscape interpretation using multiple data sources (chapter 9). This Iron Age landscape had previously been a wetland landscape, containing organic archaeological remains that had been documented previously (Whiting 1936). However, increased drainage of the local area during the 1980s led to concerns about the de-watering of the wet-preserved archaeology. These concerns were addressed through a number of separate assessment projects throughout the 1980s and early 1990s (see Parker Pearson and Sydes 1997 for an overview).

In 1997 a systematic programme was developed, aimed at assessing the likely preservation of the site following GPS survey and GIS modelling of the site. This investigation had indicated that preservation levels might be better than previously thought (Chapman and Van de Noort 2001, see chapter 9). This was similarly confirmed through an initial excavation. A programme of monitoring the shape and changes to the water table annually was consequently designed and carried out by Hull University. A grid of 50 monitoring points, using piezometers, was constructed and the water table at each point was measured every two weeks over a period of over two years (Van de Noort *et al.* 2001, Chapman and Cheetham 2002). This was undertaken in conjunction with additional excavations such that the archaeological layers containing organic material could be compared with the water table across the site to see whether it was likely to be saturated still or to be drying out. Furthermore, the modelling of these data was undertaken to enable decisions to be made about the future management of the site which was to include a programme of re-wetting through controlling the local drainage system.

The data from the piezometers at each site visit were combined in the GIS to generate a model of the shape of the top of the water, also showing the height of the water surface at different areas of the site (*51*).

This model could also be compared with a model of the landscape surface derived from GPS survey (Chapman and Van de Noort 2001). The results from

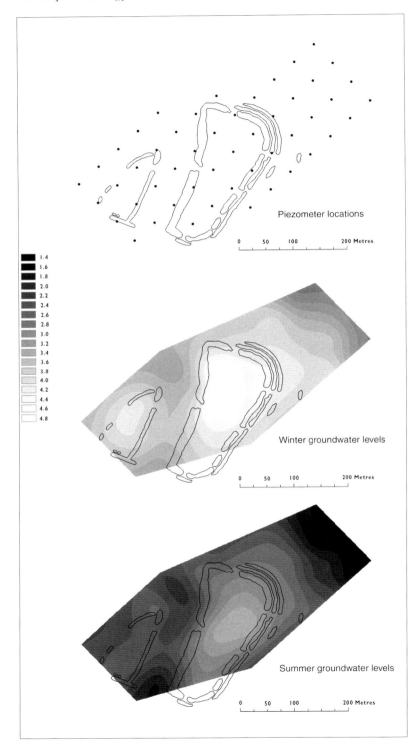

Legend values:
1.4
1.6
1.8
2.0
2.2
2.4
2.6
2.8
3.0
3.2
3.4
3.6
3.8
4.0
4.2
4.4
4.6
4.8

Piezometer locations

0   50   100   200 Metres

Winter groundwater levels

0   50   100   200 Metres

Summer groundwater levels

0   50   100   200 Metres

51 Modelling water table data at the Iron Age site of Sutton Common, South Yorkshire

the modelling of the water table were then compared to the positions where archaeological wood had been identified previously during excavations. The majority of the archaeological wood was in the form of stakes or posts providing a vertical profile of preservation levels compared with depth. Thus it was possible to compare levels of preservation vertically with the position of the fluctuating water table at each position (*colour plate 19*).

The changing water table throughout the year was divided into three blocks following modelling in the GIS. The first of these reflected areas of permanent saturation, always below the water level, indicating areas where the greatest levels of preservation were likely to be encountered. The second reflected the 'zone of fluctuation', or that area of the profile which was wet at some periods of the year but dry at others, indicating an area where organic archaeological remains were likely to be less well preserved. Finally, the third zone was one which, during the period of monitoring, was permanently dry, except for seepage through the topsoil. This area was considered to be the least well preserved. The Sutton Common landscape was then subdivided into these zones using the GIS.

By comparing the three saturation zones with the archaeological timbers it was possible to test the hypothesis relating to the relationship between saturation levels and organic preservation. The results from the modelling reflected those demonstrated by the preservation of the timbers in each location, with the best preservation displayed by the permanently saturated wood, in contrast to the permanently dry areas which displayed extremely poor preservation levels.

In terms of GIS, the results of these analyses demonstrated firstly that the water table was not flat. This provided some hope in relation to the preservation of organic archaeology on the raised 'islands' of the site, under which the water table appeared to dome upwards. Secondly, it demonstrated the fluctuations throughout the year. By calibrating the GIS model by using excavated wood, it was possible to begin to predict the likely levels of preservation elsewhere on the site. Given that the DEM of the surface existed, and that the tops of the majority of archaeological features were within 30cm of the land surface, then it became possible to predict which areas of the site were at greatest threat and which areas it might be possible to preserve in the longer term.

CONCLUSIONS

The use of GIS for cultural resource management is an extremely broad subject. In the case of landscape archaeology, and within the scope of this book, a number of key themes may be considered. Fundamentally, GIS provides an extremely useful toolbox for addressing themes of cultural resource management. This has been demonstrated with fluvial erosion and in terms of the de-watering of saturated sites. However, GIS may also provide volumetric measurements of erosion, and may enable the comparison of survey data over a number of years.

Fundamentally, the role of GIS as a tool for cultural resource management cannot be overstated. To date this has been exploited within record offices and in terms of database management. Elsewhere, approaches such as the predictive modelling of archaeological site locations has been used to great effect. Fundamentally, GIS provides a method of visualising and analysing multiple datasets together. In doing so, it becomes possible to quantify the effects of alterations to the landscape, whether from erosion, de-watering or a development. Each layer of data will have differing elements of accuracy. Thus as a modelling technique, and with the benefit of generated metadata, GIS can address issues of cultural resource management that might not be achieved using other methods.

11

GIS and illustration

INTRODUCTION

GIS may be seen as a medium for storing and managing spatial data, for examining multiple layers of data, and for performing analyses on layers of information to create new data. It has also been demonstrated that GIS may be considered as a tool for exploring data in a virtual way, to examine themes of perception and space. In each of these examples the emphasis has been on displaying and modelling data, in addition to visualising different types of information. Whilst the graphical interface of GIS provides an increasingly realistic image of landscapes, there are a number of ways in which GIS may be considered as part of a wider graphical toolkit which, together, can provide images that are more directly recognisable to a wider audience and graphically more pleasing. This may be for a number of purposes.

In the previous chapters, the various analytical capabilities of GIS have been examined. In this chapter GIS is considered as a graphical tool. Here the results of these types of analyses will be examined in relation to the various ways in which data may be presented in a more graphical form. There are no rules to approaching graphics as an output from GIS, although this chapter serves to provide some examples of how the combination of GIS software with other graphical packages can present alterative methods of presenting results. This is particularly pertinent with the recent growth in virtual reality (VR) applications within archaeology which have become increasingly popular within themes of public dissemination.

GIS, ARCHAEOLOGY AND VISUALISATION

The value of visualisation of archaeological landscapes resides largely with the ability to view multiple layers of data together in a more representative form (*colour plates 20* and *21*). For example, topography may be viewed in conjunction with aerial photography or historical mapping by draping a georeferenced image over the DEM and viewing it in three-dimensions, thus enabling correlations to be examined qualitatively as well as quantitatively (*colour plates 22* and *23*). Furthermore, analytical surfaces, such as derived slope models, often make more sense when draped over the DEM surface, enabling elevation changes to be examined in conjunction with gradient. Ultimately, by viewing DEMs in three-dimensions, the result is a clearer simulation of one's perception of the actual landscape. This experience may be further enhanced by controls such as the exaggeration of the vertical axis. In this way, the use of computer visualisation provides the capability of 'bringing the past to life' (Miller and Richards 1994).

Previously, the possibilities of visualisation within GIS have been categorised (though not exclusively) into four principal areas: (1) for the study and analysis of a Digital Terrain Model, (2) for the three-dimensional representation of different layers of raster and vector data and images, (3) for the three-dimensional overlay of all landscape data and (4) for archaeological landscape navigation in real time and at multiple resolutions (Forte 1995). This may be considered to have increased relevance due to the fact that archaeology is an extremely visual subject (Miller and Richards 1995).

The value of visualisation, however, remains one of some debate. As outlined by Miller and Richards (1995), much of the purpose of archaeological computer-based visualisation, such as through GIS, has been to present existing knowledge in a more accessible way to the public rather than to advance research priorities. However, other, perhaps more positive, values may be interpreted. For example, through the creation of a computer-based visualisation it becomes necessary to make decisions about gaps in knowledge and to thus create hypotheses. In other words, by creating a visualisation of a landscape, all regions within a study area must be considered, particularly where reconstruction is concerned. In some areas archaeological data might be readily available for reconstruction, whereas in others data might be scarce or lacking. However, the visualisation is unkind insofar as it demands that, for completeness, even these areas must be reconstructed. Thus, rather than ignore gaps in archaeological data, the visualisation process itself might begin to assist in highlighting gaps in knowledge and force the hands of researchers to generate new hypotheses that might be tested in the future.

However, as a cautionary note, it has been noted that the use of visualisation 'should carry a health warning' (Miller and Richards 1995, 21). Drawing from the use of graphics within the entertainment and advertising industries, it may be argued that the creation of such visualisations has the role of manipulating the audience. The use of visualisation, with its current primary function as a method of translating results to a wider audience, should therefore be treated with some level of responsibility. More positively, however, it has been noted that the use of archaeological visualisation within the spatial technologies provides better ways of engaging with archaeological landscapes and exploring them. With this in mind, it may be argued that the use of such 'virtual reality' within landscape archaeology may enable a more theoretically active approach to archaeological interpretation and communication compared with previous, largely static and reactive, approaches (Gillings and Goodrick 1996). Similarly, Barceló (2000) has argued that the key to making the most from virtual reality within landscape archaeology lies with creating simulations of archaeological reasoning.

2D MAPPING AND GRAPHICS

At a basic level, GIS can provide a two-dimensional visualisation of various layers of data. These may relate to distributions of artefact or sites in relation to maps, aerial photographs or the results from geophysical survey. Many GIS packages allow the coding of data such that different fields in a database may be represented using different symbols, or even by using custom-made symbols. In many ways the increased resolution and output quality of GIS packages is reducing the need for graphics software packages within many archaeological applications. However, there are a number of issues relating to the use of GIS for graphical purposes.

Using multiple rectified raster images can create visual problems when used together within a GIS. The conversion to a new raster following georeferencing forces the creation of a box of data relating to the maximum extents of the image. Effectively, this provides a minimum and maximum x and y value with the area in between being part of the model. Thus if an image is rotated, then additional space is created outside of the original extents of the image. Whilst this would normally not affect many applications of GIS, occasionally it will be necessary to view multiple georeferenced images together, such as geophysical surveys from a number of separate fields. In this case it is possible for the new extents boxes to overlap, thus hiding areas of some of the surveys. In most cases it is possible to reclassify a georeferenced images so that these additional areas become 'NoData' and are thus not represented. In other cases it becomes more useful to stitch images together using a graphics software package, based on survey information, and to re-import and georeference the combined image as a single raster.

Furthermore, in many cases, the mapping data are less visually impressive than they are useful in more analytical ways. Similarly, copyright issues can restrict the direct use of such data. In terms of translating the results of archaeological work, often an additional stage will be required. In these cases, alternatives may be used. Two principal, though related, alternatives may be provided. Either it is possible to export the resulting GIS image to a graphics package to be 'tidied up', or else it is possible to generate elements such as base maps within the graphics package to be imported and georeferenced within the GIS. The latter approach enables more 'graphical' images to be produced.

DRAPING GRAPHICAL IMAGES

Despite the increasingly realistic graphical output from GIS, presenting the results of some analyses can be visually limited. For example, in chapter 7 the concept of vegetation reconstruction was considered in relation to predicting where different vegetation types might have existed during a given period. The results from such analyses will invariably be in the form of either a series of raster layers, or as a series of polygons representing different vegetation units. Such abstract results can be difficult to communicate, particularly to a non-specialist audience.

One method for addressing this issue is to effectively convert the analytical results to an illustrative layer by using a combination of software packages. Following the generation of the analytical model it is possible to export the results as an image. By importing this image into a graphics or illustration software package, the results can effectively be 'painted' so that they become more visually readable through being more 'realistic'. Particularly through the use of textures, it is possible to render the image with appropriate representations of water, woodland types and grassland, in addition to archaeological features such as fields or routeways. Furthermore, this approach enables the resulting image to be as representative, illustrative or realistic as is appropriate or required. After the image has been generated, it can then be re-imported into the GIS and georeferenced to place it back in its correct spatial position. Once georeferenced, it can be draped over the DEM and light-shaded. The resulting model should provide a much more visually readable result compared with the traditional GIS outputs. In some GIS packages this may be further enhanced by placing three-dimensional models onto the surface to represent buildings and other structures, either using those models available within the software, or through creating them in another package (such as CAD or 3D Studio Max) and importing them (*colour plate 24*).

EXPORTING TO 3D VISUALISATION SOFTWARE

Increasingly, archaeological sites and landscapes are being presented within visualisation or Virtual Reality (VR) software, to either be explored in real time, or else to construct animations. The variety of visualisation software packages means that the ways in which data may be prepared in the GIS for exporting will vary. However, through a combination of direct data conversion and the exporting of images, it is possible to provide the basis for the construction of archaeological landscape visualisations. For example, within some GIS packages, it is possible to export to VRML (Virtual Reality Macro Language) formats which will maintain the spatial integrity of the dataset in addition to rendering information. Fundamentally, however, GIS can provide the data as a basis for generating visualisations, animations and virtual landscapes.

In terms of application, the use of these approaches is clearly extremely useful as a method of translating archaeological results to a wider audience. However, the use of such approaches could have wider reaching implications, particularly with the capability of generating different versions of the past, such as vegetation coverage, which will have clearly readable implications for interpretation. Clearly this will have an impact on the landscape approaches aimed at reconstructing the landscape (chapter 7), or on the use of landscape theory (chapter 8). From the perspective of interpretation, such an approach provides very little room for 'fudging' results, as each element of the resulting landscape needs to be effectively 'constructed' within the computer.

MAINTAINING CREDIBILITY

Making GIS and the results from GIS more visually readable and applicable to a wider audience does come with a number of potential pitfalls. At a fundamental level, these centre on issues of credibility. Often the more visually impressive a computer model is, the more likely it is to be accepted as 'correct'. Furthermore, this might be considered at high resolutions where the original GIS model was much coarser. In each case the basis of the problem lies in metadata, or data about data. In other words, it is important to ensure that any resulting visualisation is accompanied by a description of the types of data that were used to create it, including which areas are based on guess work, which are predicted and which are based on data. Similarly, it is important to note the original resolution of the model surface.

By making metadata available, it is possible for audiences to assess the validity of the data, and also to see where further work may be required. If metadata is not included, then the validity of the model will remain unknown. Through continued use of the results, the visualisation may become further divorced from the original input data such that its reliability will not be known.

CONCLUSIONS

In this chapter, various ways of generating a more graphically focused output from GIS have been examined. Whilst many GIS packages are increasing their capacity for graphical outputs at both two and three dimensions, the integration of GIS software with graphical packages provides a broader framework of potential for making the most from the GIS.

12
Final words

In chapter 1, the aim of this book was defined as to essentially provide avenues whereby the themes of landscape archaeology could be addressed using the spatial sciences and specifically Geographical Information Systems. To this end landscape archaeology was divided into three strands. The first concerned landscape analysis, defined by the characterisation of the archaeological landscape and its interpretation through the examination of natural and cultural features. The second strand focused on environmental and cultural reconstruction of the landscape, focusing on changes to the physical landscape, exploring how, through reconstruction, it is possible to enrich the interpretation of archaeological sites and landscapes. The final strand concerned the integration of theoretical approaches to interpreting archaeological landscapes and how such approaches may be incorporated within the GIS. Whilst each of these areas provides credible methods for approaching the study of archaeological landscapes, it is my belief that the true value of GIS is the potential it provides for integrating these strands together, thus providing a more holistic approach to landscape archaeology.

The structure of this book commenced with a discussion of the practicalities of using spatial data generally, and incorporating archaeological data more specifically (chapters 2-5). This included some of the issues and caveats that should be considered when using GIS for data processing and manipulation. This was followed by a consideration of the three principal themes of landscape archaeology addressing ways in which GIS may enrich current approaches and provide additional opportunities for study and analysis (chapters 6-8). Different landscape archaeology projects will have different aims and so the succeeding two chapters addressed the impact of GIS from the perspectives of landscape interpretation more broadly (chapter 9) and cultural resource management (chapter 10). Due to the use of GIS as a cartographic tool and a very visual medium, an additional chapter explored the ways in which GIS may be developed to become a part of the suite of digital illustration tools to provide greater accessibility to the results of analyses (chapter 11).

Throughout the book, a number of key themes have been continually highlighted and it is appropriate to reiterate some of these here. Primarily, data quality will always underlie the quality of any additional analyses within the GIS. Data quality not only concerns issues of accuracy such as digitising precision or coordinate deviation, but also includes database standardisation and archaeological accuracy. Secondly, themes of scale and resolution are of fundamental importance to analyses. Different datasets will be collected for use at different scales but may be visualised at a range of other scales within the GIS. This has impacts for working with both raster and vector data formats. Thirdly, the ways in which different natural and cultural features are depicted will potentially have an impact on the results of the GIS analysis. As with cartography more generally, depiction is normally appropriate to particular scales or for particular purposes. Within GIS, the translation of features into the digital space will require decisions to be made about how they will be depicted; for example, as a vector or raster file. The issues arise largely from the decision of what to omit in depiction. Will an archaeological feature be reduced to a point file, for example, and how will it be labelled? Fundamentally, the importance of acknowledging these key themes lies in the ability of GIS to both depict at all scales, regardless of input-data quality, and also to generate additional data derived from the variety of analyses. Once additional layers of data are generated it is possible to create extremely misleading results. As such it is important to stress the value of keeping accurate metadata records.

From an analytical perspective, the use of GIS also requires some appreciation of theoretical themes of determinism. One of the greatest criticisms of the spatial technologies has been the potential for generating environmentally deterministic models. Essentially, analysis of archaeological landscapes within GIS stems from the ability to examine the cultural landscape within the physical landscape in a way that is not achievable from either the paper map or from the ground. However, there may be a tendency to explain cultural patterns within the framework of observed correlation with environmental features. Such an explanation may not always be appropriate since cultural factors may have as much if not more significance in the placing of certain features. For example, the clustering of early Bronze Age monuments surrounding Stonehenge is more likely to have been determined by the proximity to earlier cultural structures than links with the natural features of the landscape.

CONTEMPORARY GIS

In 1995, Gaffney, Stančič and Watson provided an assessment of the impact of GIS on archaeology at that time (Gaffney *et al.* 1995). They cautioned that the 'unthoughtful' use of GIS could lead to much criticism, particularly on reflection of previous functionally and economically deterministic models used in archaeology. However, they noted that 'we have the opportunity to treat GIS as a "core" technology which can be developed according to our own agenda' and that 'used carefully, archaeology can only benefit from such a situation' (*Ibid.* 227). In a more recent volume, David Wheatley and Mark Gillings (2002) noted that one of the great successes of GIS had been the development of web-based discussion groups of archaeologists using spatial technologies and the abundance of shared data, knowledge and experience. Furthermore, they recognised that the growth in these technologies at a broader level had already begun to alter the ways in which archaeologists conducted all aspects of their work, from field to office. They expressed hope for a future in which this spatial technology research community would continue to grow and, through sharing, might eventually break down the discipline boundaries of 'academic, fieldworker and cultural resource manager' (*Ibid.* 245).

The interceding decade or more, since 1995, has seen the development of GIS as a 'core technology' within archaeology, which is constantly developing in the ways in which it may be used, both in isolation, and in conjunction with an ever growing suite of spatial technologies. The period since 1995 has seen the growth of GIS from workstations to personal computers, with increasingly intuitive interfaces. The result of this has been that GIS has become more accessible to a wider number of people within areas of research and curatorial archaeology. Increasingly GIS is being seen as an integral aspect of archaeological work assisting at all levels.

THE FUTURE OF GIS

The future of GIS within landscape archaeological research is difficult to define. The growth in the spatial technologies and their use within archaeology is altering the way in which data are collected in the field and how past archaeological records are being handled and archived. The boundaries between the different spatial technologies means that GIS is becoming just one of a suite of techniques that encompass all areas of archaeological work from archives, to data collection, to analysis, to illustration. This has also been exemplified by the increasing accessibility of the software to non-specialists, heralding new ways in which archaeological landscapes may be approached.

The momentum of GIS and the spatial sciences within landscape archaeology demonstrates how its use is likely to continue growing. Change for the future is most likely to be in the ways that these spatial technologies alter the ways in which archaeology is approached. Traditional themes are being broken down. A key example is the function of visualisation within landscape archaeology. A decade ago, visualisation would arguably have been the final, optional stage of research. Now, computer-based visualisation can assist in all phases of work, including site prospection, landscape analysis, interpretation and illustration. The future of GIS and the spatial sciences appears set to blur the edges between the traditional themes of landscape archaeology and to develop new agendas for its study.

Bibliography

Aldenderfer, M. 1996. Introduction, in M. Aldenderfer and H. D. G. Maschner (ed.) *Anthropology, space, and geographic information systems*, 3-18. Oxford: Oxford University Press.

Altschul, J. H. 1990. Red flag models: the use of modelling in management contexts, in K. M. S. Allen, S. W. Green and E. B. W. Zubrow (ed.) *Interpreting space: GIS and archaeology*, 226-38. London: Taylor and Francis.

Aston, M. 1985. *Interpreting the landscape. Landscape archaeology and local history*. London: BT Batsford Ltd.

Bahn, P. (ed.) 1992. *Dictionary of archaeology*. Glasgow: Harper Collins.

Barceló, J. A. 2000. Visualizing what might be. An introduction to virtual reality in archaeology, in J. A. Barceló, M. Forte and D. Sanders (ed.) *Virtual reality in archaeology*, 9-36. Oxford: BAR S843.

Beard, M. K. and Buttenfeld, B. P. 1999. Detecting and evaluating errors by graphical methods, in P. A. Longley, M. F. Goodchild, D. J. Maguire and D. W. Rhind (ed.) *Geographcial information systems, volume I* (second edition), 219-33. New York: John Wiley and Sons.

Bell, J. A. 1994. Interpretation and testability in theories about prehistoric thinking, in C. Renfrew and E. B. W. Zubrow (ed.) *The ancient mind: elements of cognitive archaeology*, 15-21. Cambridge: Cambridge University Press.

Bell, T. and Lock, G. 2000. Topographic and cultural influences on walking the Ridgeway in later prehistoric times, in G. Lock (ed.) *Beyond the map – archaeology and spatial technologies*, 85-100. Amsterdam: IOS Press.

Bender, B. 1992. Theorising landscapes, and the prehistoric landscapes of Stonehenge. *Man* 27, 735-55.

Bender, B. (ed.) 1993. *Landscapes: politics and perspectives*. Oxford: Berg.

Bender, B., Hamilton, S. and Tilley, C. 1997. Leskernick: stone worlds; alternative narratives; nested landscapes. *Proceedings of the Prehistoric Society* 63, 147-78.

Bernhardsen, T. 1992. *Geographic information systems*. Arendal: Viak IT.

Bewley, R., Donaghue, D., Gaffney, V., van Leusen, M. and Wise, A. (ed.) 1999. *Archiving aerial photography and remote sensing data*. Oxford: Oxbow: Archaeology Data Service.

Binford, L. R. 1964. A consideration of archaeological research design. *American Antiquity* 29, 425-41.

Birks, H. J. B. 1989. Holocene Isochrome maps and patterns of tree spreading in the British Isles. *Journal of Biogeography* 16, 503-40.

Birks, H. J. B. and Birks, H. H. 1980. *Quaternary palaeoecology.* London: Edward and Arnold.

Boaz, J. and Uleberg, E. 2000. Quantifying the non-quantifiable: studying hunter-gatherer landscapes, in G. Lock (ed.) *Beyond the map: archaeology and spatial technologies*, 101-15. Amsterdam: IOS Press.

Bourdieu, P. 1977. *Outline of a theory of practice.* Cambridge: Cambridge University Press.

Bradley, R. 1984. *The social foundations of prehistoric Britain; themes and variations in the archaeology of power.* London: Longman.

Bradley, R. 1993. *Altering the earth: the origins of monuments in Britain and continental Europe.* Edinburgh: Society of Antiquaries of Scotland Monograph Series No. 8.

Bradley, R. 2000. *An Archaeology of Natural Places.* London: Routledge.

Brasington, J., Rumsby, B. T., and McVey, R. A. 2000. 'Monitoring and modelling morphological change in braided river systems using the Global Positioning System'. Earth Surface Processes and Landforms, 25, 973-990.

Bowden, M. (ed.) 1999. *Unravelling the landscape. An inquisitive approach to archaeology.* Stroud: Tempus Publishing Ltd.

Burl, A. 1969. Henges: internal features and regional groups. *Archaeological Journal* 126, 1-28.

Burrough, P. A. 1986. *Principles of geographical information systems for land resources assessment.* Oxford: Clarendon Press.

Carmichael, D. L. 1990. GIS predictive modelling of prehistoric site distributions in central Montana, in K. M. S. Allen, S. W. Green and E. B. W. Zubrow (ed.) *Interpreting space: GIS and archaeology*, 216-25. London: Taylor and Francis.

Carrara, A., Bitelli, G. and Carla, R. 1997. Comparison of techniques for generating digital terrain models from contour lines. *International Journal of Geographical Information Systems* 11(5), 451-73.

Chapman, H. 2000. Understanding wetland archaeological landscapes: GIS, environmental analysis and landscape reconstruction; pathways and narratives, in G. Lock (ed.) *Beyond the map: archaeology and the spatial technologies*, 49-59. Amsterdam: IOS Press.

Chapman, H. P. 2001. Understanding and using archaeological surveys - the 'error conspiracy', in Z. Stančič and T. Veljanovski (ed.) *Computing archaeology for understanding the past - CAA2000. Computer applications and quantitative methods in archaeology. Proceedings of the 28th conference, Ljubljana, April 2000*, 19-23. Oxford: BAR International Series 931, Archaeopress.

Chapman, H. P. 2003. Rudston 'cursus A' - engaging with a Neolithic monument in its landscape setting using GIS. *Oxford Journal of Archaeology* 22, 345-56.

Chapman, H. P. 2005. Rethinking the 'cursus problem' – investigating the Neolithic landscape archaeology of Rudston, East Yorkshire, UK using GIS. *Proceedings of the Prehistoric Society* 71, 159-70.

Chapman, H. P. and Cheetham, J. L. 2002. Monitoring and modelling saturation as a proxy indicator for in situ preservation in wetlands: a GIS-based approach. *Journal of Archaeological Science* 29, 277–89.

Chapman, H. P., Fletcher, W. G. and Thomas, G. 2001. Quantifying the effects of erosion on the archaeology of intertidal environments: a new approach and its implications for their management. *Conservation and Management of Archaeological Sites* 4, 233–40.

Chapman, H. P. and Lillie, M. C. 2004. Investigating 'Doggerland' through analogy. The example of Holderness, East Yorkshire (UK), in N. Fleming (ed.) *Submarine prehistoric archaeology of the North Sea*, 65–9. York: Council for British Archaeology Research Report 141.

Chapman, H. P. and Van de Noort, R. 2001. High-resolution wetland prospection, using GPS and GIS: landscape studies at Sutton Common (South Yorkshire), and Meare Village East (Somerset). *Journal of Archaeological Science* 28, 365–75.

Charman, D. and Chambers, F. (ed.) 2004. Holocene special issue: peatlands and Holocene environmental change. *The Holocene* 14, 1–144.

Childe, V. G. 1925. *The dawn of European civilisation*. London: Routledge and Keegan Paul.

Chartrand, J., Richards, J. and Vyner, B. 1993. Bridging the urban–rural gap: GIS and the York Environs Project, in J. Andresen, T. Madsen and I. Scollar (ed.) *Computing the past: computer applications and quantitative methods in archaeology – CAA92*, 159–66. Aarhus: Aarhus University Press.

Clarke, D. 1978. *Analytical archaeology* (second edition). London: Methuen.

Claxton, J. B. 1995. Future enhancements to GIS: implications for archaeological theory, in G. Lock and Z. Stančič (ed.) *Archaeology and geographical information systems: a European perspective*, 335–48. London: Taylor and Francis.

Coles, B. 1998. Doggerland: a speculative study. *Proceedings of the Prehistoric Society* 64, 45–81.

Cosgrove, D. 1989. Geography is everywhere: culture and symbolism in human landscapes, in D. Gregory and R. Walford (ed.) *Horizons in human geography*, 118–35. Basingstoke: Macmillan.

Couclelis, H. 1999. Space, time, geography, in P. A. Longley, M. F. Goodchild, D. J. Maguire and D. W. Rhind (ed.) *Geographical information systems, volume 1* (second edition), 29–38. New York: John Wiley and Sons.

De Floriani, L. and Magillo, P. 1994. Visibility algorithms on triangulated digital terrain models. *International Journal of Geographical Information Systems* 8, 13–41.

De Floriani, L. and Magillo, P. 1999. Intervisibility on terrains, in P. A. Longley, M. F. Goodchild, D. J. Maguire and D. W. Rhind (ed.) *Geographical information systems, volume 1* (second edition), 543–56. New York: John Wiley and Sons.

De Floriani, L., Montani, C. and Scorpigno, R. 1994. Parallizing visibility computations on triangulated terrains. *International Journal of Geographical Information Systems* 8, 515–31.

Department of the Environment 1990. *Planning policy guidance: archaeology and planning (PPG16)*. London: Department of the Environment.

De Silva, M. and Pizziolo, G. 2001. Setting up a 'human calibrated' anisotropic cost-surface for archaeological landscape investigation, in Z. Stančič (ed.) *CAA 2000 – Computing archaeology for understanding the past*, 279-86. Oxford: BAR International Series 931.

Devereux, P. 1991. Three-dimensional aspects of apparent relationships between selected natural and artificial features within the topography of the Avebury complex. *Antiquity* 65, 894-8.

Dymond, D. P. 1966. Ritual monuments at Rudston, East Yorkshire, England. *Proceedings of the Prehistoric Society* 32, 86-95.

Ellis, C., Crone, A., Reilly, E. and Hughes, P. 2002. Excavation of a Neolithic wooden platform, Stirlingshire. *Proceedings of the Prehistoric Society* 68, 247-56.

ESRI 1995. *Understanding GIS. The ARC/INFO method*. New York: John Wiley and Sons Inc.

Exon, S., Gaffney, V., Yorston, R. and Woodward, A. 2001. *Stonehenge landscapes: journeys through real and imagined worlds*. Oxford: Archaeopress.

Fisher, P. F. 1992. First experiments in viewshed uncertainty: the accuracy of the viewshed area. *Photogrammetric Engineering and Remote Sensing* 57, 345-52.

Fisher, P. F. 1993. Algorithm and implementation uncertainty in viewshed analysis. *International Journal of Geographical information Systems* 7 (4), 331-47.

Fisher, P. F. 1999. Models of uncertainty in spatial data, in P. A. Longley, M. F. Goodchild, D. J. Maguire and D. W. Rhind (ed.) *Geographical information systems, volume 1* (second edition), 191-205. New York: John Wiley and Sons.

Fisher, P., Farrelly, C., Maddocks, A. and Ruggles, C. 1997. Spatial analysis of visible areas from the Bronze Age cairns of Mull. *Journal of Archaeological Science* 24, 581-92.

Fitch, S., Thomson, K. and Gaffney, V. 2005. Late Pleistocene and Holocene depositional systems and the palaeogeography of the Dogger Bank, North Sea. *Quaternary Research* 64, 185-96.

Fletcher, M. and Spicer, D. 1988. Clonehenge: an experiment with gridded and non-gridded survey data, in S. P. Q. Rahtz (ed.) *Computer and quantitative methods in archaeology*, 309-24. Oxford: BAR International Series 446(ii).

Fletcher, W., Chapman, H., Head, R., Fenwick, H., Van de Noort, R. and Lillie, M. 1999. The archaeological survey of the Humber estuary, in R. Van de Noort and S. Ellis (ed.) *Wetland heritage of the Vale of York: an archaeological survey*, 205-42. Hull: Humber Wetlands Project, University of Hull.

Forte, M. 1995. Scientific visualization and archaeological landscape: the case study of Terramara, Italy, in G. Lock and Z. Stančič (ed.) *Archaeology and geographical information systems: a European perspective*, 231-8. London: Taylor and Francis.

Fyfe, R. 2006. GIS and the application of a model of pollen deposition and dispersal: a new approach to testing landscape hypotheses using the POLLANDAL models. *Journal of Archaeological Science* 33, 483-93.

Gaffney, V. V. L., Bintliff, J. and Slapsak, B. 1991. Site formation processes and the Hvar Survey Project, Yugoslavia, in A. J. Schofield (ed.) *Interpreting artefact scatters – contributions to ploughzone archaeology*, 59-77. Oxford: Oxbow Monograph 4.

Gaffney, V. and Stančič, Z. 1991. Diodorus Siculus and the island of Hvar, Dalmatia: testing the text with GIS, in G. Lock and J. Moffett (ed.) *Computer and quantitative methods in archaeology 1991*, 113–25. Oxford: BAR International Series S577.

Gaffney, V., Stančič, Z. and Watson, H. 1995. The impact of GIS on archaeology: a personal perspective, in G. Lock and Z. Stančič (ed.) *Archaeology and geographical information systems: a European perspective*, 211–29. London: Taylor and Francis.

Gaffney, V., Z. Stančič and H. Watson 1996. Moving from catchments to cognition: tentative steps toward a larger archaeological context for GIS, in M. Aldenderfer and H. D. G. Maschner (ed.) *Anthropology, space and geographic information systems*, 132–54. Oxford: Oxford University Press.

Gaffney, V. and van Leusen, M. 1995. Postscript – GIS, environmental determinism and archaeology: a parallel text, in G. Lock and Z. Stančič (ed.) *Archaeology and geographical information systems: a European perspective*, 367–82. London: Taylor and Francis.

Gao, J. 1997. Resolution and accuracy of terrain representation by grid DEMs at a micro-scale. *International Journal of Geographical Information Science* 11(2), 199–212.

Gearey, B. R., Charman, D. J and Kent, M. 2000a. Palaeoecological evidence for the prehistoric settlement of Bodmin Moor, Cornwall, south–west England: Part I – the status of woodland and early human impacts. *Journal of Archaeological Science* 27, 423–38.

Gearey, B. R., Charman, D. J and Kent, M. 2000b. Palaeoecological evidence for the prehistoric settlement of Bodmin Moor, Cornwall, south–west England: Part II – land-use changes from the Neolithic to the present. *Journal of Archaeological Science* 27, 493–508.

Gearey, B. R. and Chapman, H. P. 2006. 'Digital gardening': an approach to simulating elements of palaeovegetation and some implications for the interpretation of prehistoric sites and landscapes, in T. L. Evans and P. Daly (ed.) *Digital Archaeology – bridging method and theory*, 171–90. Oxford: Routledge

Gell, A. 1985. How to read a map: remarks on the practical logic of navigation. *Man* 20, 271–86.

Gibson, J. J. 1986. *The ecological approach to visual perception*. New Jersey: Lawrence Erlbaum Associates Inc.

Gillings, M. 1995. Flood dynamics and settlement in the Tisza valley of north–east Hungary: GIS and the upper Tisza project, in G. Lock and Z. Stančič (ed.) *Archaeology and geographical information systems: a European perspective*, 67–84. London: Taylor and Francis.

Gillings, M. and Goodrick, G. T. 1996. Sensuous and reflexive GIS: exploring visualisation and VRML. *Internet Archaeology* 1, 5.1.

Gillings, M. and Wise, A. (ed.) 1999. *GIS guide to good practice*. Oxford: Oxbow and the Archaeology Data Service.

Glob, P. V. 1998. *The bog people. Iron Age man preserved*. London: Faber and Faber.

Godwin, H. 1975. *History of the British Flora. A factual basis for phytogeography*. Cambridge: Cambridge University Press.

Goucher, K. 1997. Hill of Tara topographical survey and mapping, in C. Newman, *Tara: an archaeological survey* 245-52. Dublin: Discovery Programme Monograph 2.

Guillot, D. and Leroy, G. 1995. The use of GIS for archaeological resource management in France: the SCALA project, with a case study in Picardie, in G. Lock and Z. Stančič (ed.) *Archaeology and geographical information systems: a European perspective,* 15-26. London: Taylor and Francis.

Haigh, J. G. B. 1993. Practical experience in creating digital terrain models, in J. Andresen, T. Madsen and I. Scollar (ed.) *Computing the past. Computer applications and quantitative methods in archaeology. CAA92,* 67-74. Aarhus: Aarhus University Press.

Harris, T. M. 1986. Geographic Information System design for archaeological site information retrieval, in S. Laflin (ed.) *Computer applications in archaeology 1986,* 148-61. Birmingham: University of Birmingham.

Harris, T. M. 1988. Digital terrain modelling and three-dimensional surface graphics for landscape and site analysis in archaeology and regional planning, in C. L. N. Ruggles and S. P. Q. Rahtz (ed.) *Computer applications and quantitative methods in archaeology 1987,* 161-72. Oxford: BAR International Series 393.

Harris, T. M. and Lock, G. R. 1990. The diffusion of a new technology: a perspective on the adoption of geographic information systems within UK archaeology, in K. M. S. Allen, S. W. Green and E. B. W. Zubrow (ed.) *Interpreting space: GIS and archaeology,* 33-53. London: Taylor and Francis.

Harris, T. M. and Lock, G. R. 1995. Toward an evaluation of GIS in European archaeology: the past, present and future of theory and applications, in G. Lock and Z. Stančič (ed.) *Archaeology and geographical information systems: a European perspective,* 349-65. London: Taylor and Francis.

Hasenstab, R. J. and Resnick, B. 1990. GIS in historical predictive modelling: the Fort Drum project, in K. M. S. Allen, S. W. Green and E. B. W. Zubrow (ed.) *Interpreting space: GIS and archaeology,* 284-306. London: Taylor and Francis.

Havinga, A. J. 1984. A 20 year experimental investigation into the differential corrosion susceptibility of pollen and spores in various soil types. *Pollen et Spores* 26, 541-58.

Heuvelink, G. B. M. 1999. Propagation of error in spatial modelling with GIS, in P. A. Longley, M. F. Goodchild, D. J. Maguire and D. W. Rhind (ed.) *Geographical information systems, volume 1* (second edition), 207-17. New York: John Wiley and Sons.

Higuchi, T. 1983. *Visual and spatial structure of landscapes.* Massachusetts, MIT.

Hoskins, W. G. 1955. *The making of the English landscape.* London: Hodder and Stoughton.

Hutchinson, M. F. and Gallant, J. C. 1999. Representation of terrain, in P. A. Longley, M. F. Goodchild, D. J. Maguire and D. W. Rhind (ed.) *Geographical information systems, volume 1* (second edition), 105-24. New York: John Wiley and Sons.

Ingold, T. 2000. *The perception of the environment: essays on livelihood, dwelling and skill.* London: Routledge.

João, E. M. 1998. *Causes and consequences of map generalisation.* London: Taylor and Francis.

Johnson, M. 1999. *Archaeological theory.* Oxford: Blackwell Publishers Ltd.

Kohler, T. A. and Parker, S. C. 1986. Predictive models for archaeological resource location, in M. B. Schiffer (ed.) *Advances in archaeological method and theory*, volume 9, 397-452. New York: Academic Press.

Kuna, M. and Adelsbergerová, D. 1995. Prehistoric location preferences: an application of GIS to the Vinorský potok project, Bohemia, the Czech Republic, in G. Lock and Z. Stančič (ed.) *Archaeology and geographical information systems: a European perspective*, 117-31. London: Taylor and Francis.

Kvamme, K. L. 1990. GIS algorithms and their effect on regional archaeological analysis, in K. M. A. Allen, S. W. Green and E. B. W. Zubrow (ed.) *Interpreting space: GIS and archaeology*, 112-25. London: Taylor and Francis.

Kvamme, K. L. 1992. Terrain form analysis of archaeological location through geographic information systems, in G. Lock and J. Moffett (ed.) *Computer applications and quantitative methods in archaeology 1991*, 127-36. Oxford: BAR International Series S577.

Kyriakidis, P.C., Shortridge, A. M. and Goodchild, M. 1999. Geostatistics for conflation and accuracy assessment of digital elevation models. *International Journal of Geographical Information Science* 13, 677-707.

Lake, M. W., Woodman, P. E. and Mithen, S. J. 1998. Tailoring GIS software for archaeological applications: an example concerning viewshed analysis. *Journal of Archaeological Science* 25, 27-38.

Leese, M. 1991. A preliminary statistical survey, in I. M. Stead, *Iron Age cemeteries in East Yorkshire*, 171-8. London: English Heritage archaeological report 22.

Li, Z. 1994. A comparative study of the accuracy of digital terrain models (DTMs) based on various data models. *Journal of Photogrammetry and Remote Sensing* 49, 2-11.

Llobera, M. 1996. Exploring the topography of mind: GIS, social space and archaeology. *Antiquity* 70, 612-22.

Llobera, M. 2001. Building past landscape perception with GIS: understanding topographic prominence. *Journal of Archaeological Science* 28, 1005-14.

Lock, G. R. and Harris, T. M. 1996. Danebury revisited: an English Iron Age hillfort in a digital landscape, in M. Aldenderfer and H. D. G. Maschner (ed.) *Anthropology, space, and geographic information systems*, 214-40. Oxford: Oxford University Press.

Long, A. J., Innes, J. B., Kirby, J. R., Lloyd, J. M., Rutherford, M. M., Shennan, I. and Tooley, M. J. 1998. Holocene sea-level change and coastal evolution in the Humber estuary, eastern England: an assessment of rapid coastal change. *The Holocene* 8, 229-47.

López, C. 1997. Locating some types of random errors in Digital Terrain Models. *International Journal of Geographical Information Science* 11(7), 677-98.

Loveday, R. 1985. *cursuses and related monuments of the British Neolithic*. Leicester: Unpublished PhD.

Madry, S. L. H. and Rakos, L. 1996. Line-of-sight and cost-surface techniques for regional research in the Arroux river valley, in H. D. G. Maschner (ed.) *New methods, old problems – geographic information systems in modern archaeological research*, 104-26. Illinois: Center for Archaeological Investigations, Southern Illinois University at Carbondale, occasional paper 23.

Marozas, B. A. and Zack, J. A. 1990. GIS and archaeological site location, in K. M. S. Allen, S. W. Green and E. B. W. Zubrow (ed.) *Interpreting space: GIS and archaeology*, 165-72. London: Taylor and Francis.

Maschner, H. D. G. 1996. The politics of settlement choice on the northwest coast: cognition, GIS, and coastal landscapes, in M. Aldenderfer and H. D. G. Maschner (ed.) *Anthropology, space, and geographic information systems*, 175-89. Oxford: Oxford University Press.

McGrail, S. 1987. *Ancient boats in North-West Europe. The archaeology of water transport to AD 1500*. London; Longman.

Meinig, D. W. 1979. The beholding eye. Ten versions of same scene, in D. W. Meinig (ed.) *The interpretation of ordinary landscapes – geographical essays*, 33-48. Oxford: Oxford University Press.

Middleton, R. and Winstanley, D. 1993. GIS in a landscape archaeology context, in J. Andresen, T. Madsen and I. Scollar (ed.) *Computing the past: computer applications and quantitative methods in archaeology 1992*, 151-8. Aarhus: Aarhus University Press.

Miller, P. and Richards, J. 1995. The good, the bad, and the downright misleading: archaeological adoption of computer visualisation, in J. Huggett and N. Ryan (ed.) *Computer applications and quantitative methods in archaeology 1994*, 19-22. Oxford: BAR International Series 600.

Muir, R. 2000. The new reading the landscape. *Fieldwork in landscape history*. Exeter: University of Exeter Press.

Nackaerts, K., Govers, G. and Van Orshoven, J. 1999. Accuracy assessment of probabilistic visibilities. *International Journal of Geographical Information Science* 13, 709-21.

Needham, J. 1971. *Science and civilisation in China*. Cambridge: Cambridge University Press.

Nunez, M., Vikkula, A. and Kirkinen, T. 1995. Perceiving time and space in an isostatically rising region, in G. Lock and Z. Stančič (ed.) *Archaeology and geographical information systems: a European perspective*, 141-51. London: Taylor and Francis.

Oakley, J. 1977. Inference, navigation and cognitive maps, in P. N. Johnson-Laird and P. C. Wason (ed.) *Thinking – readings in cognitive science,* 537-41. Cambridge: Cambridge University Press.

Olwig, K. R. 1993. Sexual cosmology: nation and landscape at the conceptual interstices of nature and culture; or, what does landscape really mean, in B. Bender (ed.) *Landscape: politics and perspectives*, 307-43. Oxford: BERG.

Ordnance Survey 1973. *Field archaeology in Great Britain*. Southampton: Ordnance Survey.

Parker Pearson, M. and Sydes, R. E. 1997. The Iron Age enclosures and prehistoric landscape of Sutton Common, South Yorkshire. *Proceedings of the Prehistoric Society* 63, 221-59.

Penny, A. and Wood, J. E. 1973. The Dorset cursus complex – a Neolithic astronomical observatory? *Archaeological Journal* 130, 44-76.

Peuker, T. K., Fowler, R. J., Little, J. J. and Mark, D. M. 1978. The triangular irregular network. *Proceedings of the DTM Symposium, American Society of Photogrammetry – American Congress on Survey and Mapping*, 24-31. St Louis, Missouri.

Piggott, S. 1968. *Ancient Europe*. Edinburgh: Edinburgh University Press.

Popper, K. 1992. *The logic of scientific discovery* (re-print). London: Routledge.

Potts, R., Jorstad, T. and Cole, D. 1996. The role of GIS in the interdisciplinary investigations at Olorgesailie, Kenya, a Pleistocene archaeological locality, in M. Aldenderfer and H. D. G. Maschner (ed.) *Anthropology, space, and geographic information systems*, 202-13. Oxford: Oxford University Press.

Pryor, F. 1991. *Flag Fen: prehistoric Fenland centre*. London: BT Batsford Ltd/English Heritage.

Punter, J.V. 1982. Landscape aesthetics: a synthesis and critique, in J. R. Gold and J. Burgess (ed.) *Valued environments*, 100-23. London: George Allen and Unwin.

Puppo, E. and P. Marzano 1997. Discrete visibility problems and graph algorithms. *International Journal of Geographical Information Systems* 11, 139-61.

Rackham, O. 1986. *The history of the countryside*. London: JM Dent and sons.

Raftery, B. 1996. *Trackway excavations in the Mountdillon bogs, Co. Longford 1985-1991*. Dublin: Irish Archaeological Wetland Unit, University College, Dublin.

Riley, D. N. 1944. The technique of air-archaeology. *Archaeological Journal* 101, 1-16.

Riley, D. N. 1980. *Early landscape from the air - studies of crop marks in South Yorkshire and North Nottinghamshire*. Sheffield: Department of Prehistory and Archaeology, University of Sheffield.

Riley, D. N. 1982. *Aerial archaeology in Britain*. Princes Risborough: Shire Publications Ltd.

Riley, D. N. 1988. Air survey of Neolithic sites on the Yorkshire Wolds, in T. G. Manby (ed.) *Archaeology in eastern Yorkshire, essays in honour of T.C.M. Brewster*, 89-93. Sheffield: Department of Archaeology and Prehistory, University of Sheffield.

Ruggles, C. L. N., Medyckyj-Scott, D. J. and Gruffydd, A. 1993. Multiple viewshed analysis using GIS and its archaeological application: a case study in northern Mull, in J. Andresen, T. Madsen and I. Scollar (ed.) *Computing the past: computer applications and quantitative methods in archaeology 1993*, 125-31. Aarhus: Aarhus University Press.

Salter, M. 1992. *The castles and moated mansions of Warwickshire*. Malvern: Folly Publications.

Savage, S. H. 1990. GIS in archaeological research, in K. M. S. Allen, S. W. Green and E. B. W. Zubrow (ed.) *Interpreting space: GIS and archaeology*, 22-32. London: Taylor and Francis.

Spikins, P. 2000. GIS models of past vegetation: an example from northern England, 10,000-5000 BP. *Journal of Archaeological Science* 27, 219-34.

Stead, I. M. 1991. *Iron Age cemeteries in east Yorkshire*. London: English Heritage Archaeological Report 22.

Stead, S. 1995. Humans and PETS in space, in G. Lock and Z. Stančič (ed.) *Archaeology and geographical information systems: a European perspective*, 313-7. London: Taylor and Francis.

Stine, R. S. and Lanter, D. P., 1990. Considerations for archaeology database design, in K. M. S. Allen, S. W. Green and E. B. W. Zubrow (ed.) *Interpreting space: GIS and archaeology*, 80-9. London: Taylor and Francis.

Stoertz, C. 1997. *Ancient landscapes of the Yorkshire Wolds: aerial photographic transcription and analysis.* Swindon: RCHME.

Taylor, C. 1984. *Village and farmstead. A history of rural settlement in England.* London: George Philip.

Thomas, J. 1993. The politics of vision and the archaeologies of landscape, in B. Bender (ed.) *Landscape: politics and perspectives,* 19-48. Oxford: Berg.

Tilley, C. 1994. *A phenomenology of landscape - places, paths and monuments.* Oxford: Berg.

Tilley, C. 1996. The powers of rocks: topography and monument construction on Bodmin Moor. *World Archaeology* 28, 161-176.

Tschan, A. P., Raczkowski, W. and Latalowa, M. 2000. Perception and viewsheds: are they mutually inclusive? In G. Lock (ed.) *Beyond the map: archaeology and the spatial technologies,* 28-48. Amsterdam: IOS Press.

Tuan, Y-F. 1977. *Space and place. The perspective of experience.* London: Edward Arnold Ltd.

Tuan, Y-F. 1979. Thought and landscape. The eye and the mind's eye, in D. W. Meinig (ed.) *The interpretation of ordinary landscapes - geographical essays,* 89-102. Oxford: Oxford University Press.

Turner, R. C. and Scaife, R. G. 1995. *Bog bodies: new discoveries and new perspectives.* London: British Museum Press.

Van de Noort, R., Chapman, H. P. and Cheetham, J. L. 2001. *In situ* preservation as a dynamic process: the example of Sutton Common, UK. *Antiquity* 75, 94-100.

Van de Noort, R. and Ellis, S. (ed.) 1995. *Wetland heritage of Holderness: an archaeological survey.* Hull: Humber Wetlands Project, University of Hull.

Van de Noort, R. and Ellis, S. (ed.) 1997. *Wetland heritage of the Humberhead Levels: an archaeological survey.* Hull: Humber Wetlands Project, University of Hull.

Van de Noort, R. and Ellis, S. (ed.) 1998. *Wetland heritage of the lower Trent and Ancholme valleys: an archaeological survey.* Hull: Humber Wetlands Project, University of Hull.

Van de Noort, R. and Ellis, S. (ed.) 1999. *Wetland heritage of the Vale or York: an archaeological survey.* Hull: Humber Wetlands Project, University of Hull.

Van de Noort, R. and Ellis, S. (ed.) 2000. *Wetland heritage of the Hull valley: an archaeological survey.* Hull: Humber Wetlands Project, University of Hull.

Van de Noort, R. and Powelsland, D. 2001. *Managing the wetlands in England – a GIS-resource for curators.* Exeter: University of Exeter.

Van der Knapp, W. G. M. 1992. The vector to raster conversion: (mis)use in geographical information systems. *International Journal of Geographical Information Systems* 6(2), 159-70.

Van Leusen, P. M. 1993. Cartographic modelling in a cell-based GIS, in J. Andresen, T. Madsen and I. Scollar (ed.) *Computing the past: computer applications and quantitative methods in archaeology (CAA92),* 105-23. Aarhus: Aarhus University Press.

Van Leusen, P. M. 1995. GIS and archaeological resource management: a European agenda, in G. Lock and Z. Stančič (ed.) *Archaeology and geographical information systems: a European perspective,* 27-41. London: Taylor and Francis.

Van Leusen, M. 1999. Viewshed and cost-surface analysis using GIS (cartographic modelling in a cell-based GIS II), in J. A. Barcelo, I. Briz and A. Vila (ed.) *CAA98: New techniques for old times – doing archaeology today for tomorrow society*. Oxford: BAR International Series 757.

Veregin, H. 1999. Data quality parameters, in P. A. Longley, M. F. Goodchild, D. J. Maguire and D. W. Rhind (ed.) *Geographical information systems, volume 1* (second edition), 177-89. New York: John Wiley and Sons.

Verhagen, P. 1996. The use of GIS as a tool for modeling ecological change, in H. Kamermans and K. Fennema (ed.) *Interfacing the past – CAA95* volume 1, 317-24. Leiden: University Press.

Voigtmann, A., Becker, L. and Hinrichs, K. 1997. A hierarchical model for multiresolution surface reconstruction. *Graphical Models and Image Processing* 59(5), 333-48.

Wainwright, J. and Thornes, J. B. 1991. Computer hardware modeling of archaeological sediment transport on hillslopes, in K. Lockyear and S. Rahtz (ed.) *CAA90 – Computer applications and quantitative methods in archaeology 1990*, 183-94. Oxford: BAR International Series 565.

Warren, R. E. 1990a. Predictive modelling in archaeology: a primer, in K. M. S. Allen, S. W. Green and E. B. W. Zubrow (ed.) *Interpreting space: GIS and archaeology*, 90-111. London: Taylor and Francis.

Warren, R. E. 1990b. Predictive modelling of archaeological site location: a case study in the Midwest, in K. M. S. Allen, S. W. Green and E. B. W. Zubrow (ed.) *Interpreting space: GIS and archaeology*, 201-15. London: Taylor and Francis.

Westcott, K. L. and Brandon, R. J. (ed.) 2000. *Practical applications of GIS for archaeologists. A predictive modeling toolkit*. London: Taylor and Francis.

Wheatley, D. 1993. Going over old ground: GIS, archaeological theory and the act of perception, in J. Andresen, T. Madsen and I. Scollar (ed.) *Computer applications and quantitative methods in archaeology, CAA'92*, 133-8. Aahus: Aarhus University Press.

Wheatley, D. 1995. Cumulative viewshed analysis: a GIS-based method for investigating intervisibility, and its archaeological application, in G. Lock and Z. Stančič (ed.) *Archaeology and geographical information systems: a European perspective*, 171-85. London: Taylor and Francis.

Wheately, D. 1996. The use of GIS to understand regional variation in earlier Neolithic Wessex, in H. D. G. Maschner (ed.) *New methods, old problems – geographic information systems in modern archaeological research*, 75-103. Illinois: Center for Archaeological Investigations, Southern Illinois University at Carbondale, occasional paper 23.

Wheatley, D. and Gillings, M. 2000. Vision, perception and GIS: developing enriched approaches to the study of archaeological visibility, in G. Lock (ed.) *Beyond the map: archaeology and spatial technologies*, 1-27. Amsterdam: IOS Press.

Wheatley, D. and Gillings, M. 2002. *Spatial technology and archaeology. The archaeological applications of GIS*. London: Taylor and Francis.

Whiting, C. E. 1936. Excavations at Sutton Common 1933, 1934 and 1935. *Yorkshire Archaeological Journal* 33, 57-80.

Williams, I., Limp, W. F. and Briuer, F. L. 1990. Using geographic information systems and exploratory data analysis for archaeological site classification and analysis, in K. M. S. Allen, S. W. Green and E. B. W. Zubrow (ed.) *Interpreting space: GIS and archaeology,* 239-73. London: Taylor and Francis.

Wilson, D. R. 1982. *Air photo interpretation for archaeologists.* London: BT Batsford Ltd.

Wood, E. S. 1963. *Collins field guide to archaeology in Britain.* London: Collins.

Wood, J. D. and Fisher, P. F. 1993. Assessing interpolation accuracy in elevation models. *Computer Graphics and Applications* 13, 48-56.

Wright, E.V. 1990. *The Ferriby boats: seacraft of the Bronze Age.* London: Routledge.

Wright, E.V. and Churchill, D. M. 1965. The boats from North Ferriby, Yorkshire, England, with a review of the origins of sewn plank boats of the Bronze Age. *Proceedings of the Prehistoric Society* 31, 1-30.

Wright, E.V., Hedges, R. E. M., Bayliss, A. and Van de Noort, R. 2001. New AMS radiocarbon dates for the North Ferriby boats – a contribution to dating prehistoric seafaring in northwestern Europe. *Antiquity* 75, 726-34.

Wright, E.V., Hutchinson, G. R. and Gregson, C. W. 1989. A fourth boat-find at North Ferriby, Humberside. *Archaeological Journal* 147, 44-57.

Wright, E.V. and Switsur, V. R. 1993. The Ferriby 5 boat fragment. *Yorkshire Archaeological Journal* 75, 726-34.

Wright, C. W. and Wright, E.V. 1939. Submerged boat at North Ferriby. *Antiquity* 13, 349-54.

Wright, E.V. and Wright, C. W. 1947. Prehistoric boats from North Ferriby, East Yorkshire. *Proceedings of the Prehistoric Society* 13, 114-38.

Zubrow, E. B. W. 1990a. Contemplating space: a commentary on theory, in K. M. S. Allen, S. W. Green and E. B. W. Zubrow (ed.) *Interpreting space: GIS and archaeology,* 6-72. London: Taylor and Francis.

Zubrow, E. B. W. 1990b. Modelling and prediction with geographic information systems: a demographic example from prehistoric and historic New York, in K. M. S. Allen, S. W. Green and E. B. W. Zubrow (ed.) *Interpreting space: GIS and archaeology,* 307-18. London: Taylor and Francis.

Zubrow, E. B. W. 1994. Knowledge, representation and archaeology: a cognitive example using GIS, in C. Renfrew and E. B. W. Zubrow (ed.) *The ancient mind – elements of cognitive archaeology,* 107-118. Cambridge: Cambridge University Press.

Index

If you are interested in purchasing other books published by Tempus,
or in case you have difficulty finding any Tempus books in your local bookshop,
you can also place orders directly through our website

www.tempus-publishing.com